Introduction

The cover of my book represents, hopefully, your readiness to take a friendly delving. Actually, the animal is a pooka, an imaginary disruptive friend able to enjoy life and all it imparts. Let us, together, delve down the rabbit hole.

Since the thrust of my book revolves around a violent upside for Bitcoin's price, I place a symbol ($$$) at the beginning of certain paragraphs to alert you to the forces that will add to the proposition of Bitcoin's Violent Upside. If any one paragraph is temporarily over your head, jump ahead to the next paragraph. The main thrust of my thesis is to show that BITCOIN will grow faster and faster based on market dynamics scattered throughout this book. I will do my best to contrast this with traditional finance or prevailing views. Bitcoin will not only rise to well over a million dollars per Bitcoin but will no longer be priced in dollars. In the near future, Bitcoin will only keep going up until it absorbs the world's finances as a store of wealth and value in what I expect will be the worlds only working money model.

This book will be a journey from the perspective of its author, HH.

While I try to incorporate many ideas and facets surrounding Bitcoin, I find myself agitated that it is not a complete work; I constantly want to add things and must back off. The target audience may be broad, but I write in such a way as to allow most to understand it as a broad-stroked painting. You may miss references or might not understand the essential inner workings of Bitcoin itself. Don't worry, be happy. On the other hand, I have not incorporated the more complex trains of thought so as to assuage the new to Bitcoin from yawning. I will, in all likelihood, write a part deux just for you. Be assured that wherever you are in your Bitcoin journey, you will come away with a better appreciation for Bitcoin. My commentary on the disclaimer above is rather short. Pfffftt

BITCOIN'S VIOLENT UPSIDE

Navigating the treacherous waters of untold wealth

By HARVEY HALVING

BITCOIN'S VIOLENT UPSIDE

TOPIC HEADINGS

Bitcoin's Violent Upside

First, let me congratulate you. You probably wouldn't be reading this unless you were interested in what Bitcoin was, is, and will be. Come with me optimistically down this rabbit hole. You will have trouble learning what good money is if you bring your old perceptions of money. I am here to provide you with the confidence to look at money in a new way. The content in this volume does not provide many basic fundamentals, it provides context. Even if you never heard about Bitcoin you will walk away with a new sense of adventure and reinvigorated faith in your financial future.

For a pleasant and effective reading experience, I would ask you the reader, to utilize suspended disbelief; as you might, while watching the "Roadrunner cartoon," as the Coyote, finds himself off the edge of a cliff and marvelously stays suspended in midair for several seconds; before his disastrous realization. The roadrunner *is* Bitcoin. I ask this because, and hold this number in your thinking for a while...5 BILLION percent is the percent increase Bitcoin has increased over its short lifespan.

As I proceed through the thesis of this book, I will give short summaries of information such as the meaning of money or a short history. So, down the rabbit hole we go.

The Real Meaning of Inflation

Inflation affects us all very dramatically and keeps us surreptitiously in slavery as we all strive to grasp an illusory golden ring.

As a child I would ride the carousel; a grand carnival ride with masterly painted, carved horses and various other animals. You could ride the outer horses and grasp the pole and if the horse were in the proper cycle of up and down you could barely reach the ring feeder on the outside edge of the carousel as it went round and round. Once in a while you could snatch the ring, only to discover that it was sadly, iron. After several passes and a lucky capture, the rings were all of similar color, pitch iron. One of the big benefits of taking this ride was the promise of acquiring the golden ring which would give the bearer another proud, free ride on the carousel again. This was this entrepreneur's budding view and analogy for business life ahead for me.

The golden ring was then exchanged for another ride. The value of this extra ride was almost nothing, as there were typically always plenty of extra horses to be ridden. Maybe, even there was a benefit to the carousel owner to show that the carousel was more popular than it really was. I hope you see the carousel of life that we all ride for what it is.

We reach for the golden ring, a dream fulfilled; a car, a home, a family and *insert your desire here*, which can all be had for the chasing of a few dollars. Please note that you can extract from the word dollars, the word doll or idol, a thing to be idolized or worshiped.

Be it dollars or pesos or lira, et al, there is a commonality the world over as money. Unfortunately, fiat money does not work well. It only works to keep our blinder-clad eyes on the prize; not what is going on behind the curtain. It is fiat; which is Latin for *money by decree*. This perverted relationship our government offers us is a slave-ship by their decree. Don't get me wrong governments do provide benefits to society at large such as giving us standards. Standards of laws guide our acceptable behavior by consensus. Also borders allow us to associate with whom we prefer and certain foreigners we would prefer to keep out; those who might pervert our country's mores and morals. I refrain from commenting on whether they are doing a good job or not.

The universal reason money does not work well is a simple concept that has been mystifying and confounding for all who use it. This is an act of prestidigitation, this performance of skill in magic or conjuring with sleight of hand, is simply... INFLATION.

INFLATION is printing of money. I will say it again for emphasis.

INFLATION is printing of money. Now digitally, but still, printing of money.

It is not as the Federal Reserve would have you believe; an increasing prices of goods bladity bladity, and its aggregate function yaddy yaddy, wage inferred thing that you have grown up with and have had ingrained in our collective conscious.

INFLATION is printing of money. Period. Like inflating a balloon until it pops. The popping here would represent hyperinflation.

Once digested, this will help make your financial life much easier to understand; since all FIAT MONEY has demons attached to it. One of the strongest and most vexatious of demons is called INFLATION.

Inflation will rob you blind, not at gunpoint but with your passive permission. Inflation will take more from you than any income tax, sales tax, excise tax or mugger on the street. Over a long enough time, it will take all of your hard-earned wealth. If your eyes are glazing over as I say the word "inflation," just replace it with the word "counterfeit," or I should say, endless sanctioned counterfeit. I will get into this more later on....

Gold

Physical Gold to be used as an exemplary non-fiat money and still is to a point. That point is, that no one feels able to physically buy a cart of groceries with a gold coin. To gold's credit, gold does not carry with it a yeast or that vexatious inflation. So the powers-that-be have contaminated gold by creating a fiat version of it, to make it more convenient to use and store. And here is the real evil, all of us have done nothing to stop it, even to the point of perpetuating this evil by buying paper gold (which is a derivative of gold) to our own detriment. The derivative of gold is whipped up, so as to keep its' price on the market low, but generally in pace with inflation. This is done so as not to show up the dollar by jumping to; for the sake of argument, $50,000 per ounce. This would allow for mockery of the dollar. Let me be clear: if gold rose to $50,000 per ounce, which would probably be a fairer valuation of gold, dollars would be exposed as weak and impotent in the guts of the users of dollars. There would not necessarily be a direct awareness that dollars are rendered emasculated. But it would pose a significant psychological risk to the dollar racket.

There is a better system that works flawlessly; one better than you have been used to. A Bitcoin system that conveniently does commerce, literally with a phone, it is here working securely and instantly, TODAY!

"Manipulators"

The powers-that-be are agents that do the will of a system of demons starting with the Federal Reserve Bank (FED) and other lesser central banks. This system spreads its wings out so wide to regional banks and beyond. Since governments derive power from these agencies; they sleep together and are beholden to each other. I will lump them together into an entity I will now and here forth call them, "Manipulators."

Without further explanation, there are others in the agencies of manipulators, and I will only name some of them rather than explain them. They are entities such as the IMF (International Monetary Fund), the BIS (Bank of International Settlement), and those attending Davos, those partying in the Bohemian Grove, The IRS, OECD, WTO, FSB and many others. Generally, these actors first sneered at, and now battle Bitcoin to no avail. They now realize the futility of trying to beat Bitcoin. They are currently taking the posture of closing, or limiting, the on and off-ramps to Bitcoin by using (KYC) Know Your Customer.

Bitcoiners generally prefer to refrain from interacting with manipulators and the state, but manipulators and statists want to contend with Bitcoin.

Power Shift

While Bitcoin is causing a power shift at the federal level of the US government, including the SEC, CFTC, Fin CEN, OCC, Congress, and other agency rulers, there has been a muted procession through state institutions. This resulted in attempted or enacted policies affecting Bitcoin and the people who advocate and defend Bitcoin's innovation.

It is worth understanding how these United States deal with Bitcoin's assent. These legislative assaults do not affect the Bitcoin protocol itself but rather how an individual citizen will be able to perceive or interact with the Bitcoin protocol, bearing in mind that Bitcoin holds consensus as a tenet of its mechanism. This consensus mechanism is also applied to dollars with guns and the force of law behind those dollars. The implication is that Bitcoin needs no law or the threat of firearms jammed in our faces to maintain our natural respect and need for good money.

Several states, such as Montana, Wyoming, New Hampshire, Texas, and others, have embraced Bitcoin activities.

Other butt-kissing states have fought it tooth and nail and restrict it, such as New York and Hawaii.

"Manipulators" feed us from birth, rendering us unable to think for ourselves. A shroud of delusion keeps us from first principles. They school us not to think but produce goose steppers who imagine that choice is our birthright. The clear-headed thinkers are what they fear the most.

These "Manipulators" hate Bitcoin because it removes their power to keep you in delusion and continually reallocate your money. Bitcoin is a curse to the demented dollar's status quo and all other fiat currencies, which empowers the respective governments' ability to wield power. The hundreds of trillions of dollars and other fiat systems throughout the world fear Bitcoin as a macroeconomic wrecking ball.

I am writing to the Bitcoin skeptic, all the way to the Bitcoin maximalist; either way, I want you, the reader, to utilize your superhero curiosity and put on your suspended disbelief hat for this read. This will free your mind to the journey of possibilities, no scratch that, the inevitability of the gift from God called Bitcoin.

Bitcoin is math, and **Satoshi Nakamoto** himself would tell you that he did not invent it but merely discovered it.

I hope to walk with you, talk with you, and put you on the road to Bitcoin awareness. Quite simply, Bitcoin represents a powerful alternative to your slavery. A slavery, which may be scarcely perceivable to you right now, even though it envelops your world.

That slavery is your perception of the economic world around you and how you comprehend and interact with it, how you are truly in a rats maze with no exit and no cheese. Dear reader, I want to remove you from the rat's labyrinth and lead you directly to the cheese.

To the cheese!

Bitcoin is the world's dominant monetary network right now and is growing exponentially.

Now you might say, OK, what does that mean to me? Well, Bitcoin will appreciate thousands of times from here, vanquishing the dilemma you wake up to each morning, should you own some. The struggle to cover your nut consists of purchasing sustenance, paying rent, life's necessities and taxes; oh yes, I said it, TAXES. Taxes are a considerable expense indeed. There are hundreds of taxes which I shall briefly name but a few: Income tax, sales tax, excise tax, the harmless one cent tax, which means 1% of your income, tolls, cell phone taxes, insurance is a tax, Corporate Tax twice, Sales Tax and Value Added Tax (VAT), Property taxes, Capital Gains Tax, Inheritance Tax, Estate Tax twice, Payroll Tax, Social Security tax, Medicare Tax, Excise Tax, fuel Tax, luxury Tax, Customs Duty and Tariffs, Sin Tax, Gift Tax, Assets Tax, Road Usage Tax, fuel taxes, Environmental Taxes, carbon taxes, Wealth Tax, and dare I say it...Inflation is the most insidious of all the taxes. I could fill 20 more pages of taxes. This is the perpetual entrapment in which we rats race.

But wait, there's more: Data surveillance on you and government seizure; look up CIVIL ASSET FORFEITURE. It is insidious and pervasive. Not only will Bitcoin eliminate these, but it will provide permissionless freedom to spend these funds without a third-party intermediary, and many more liberties throughout, as you read on.

My Thesis Introduction

My thesis, woven throughout this book, is the notion that Bitcoin's value will not only rise, but will eventually stabilize, offering a pathway to financial freedom. Despite its volatility, the demand for Bitcoin will shift from a mere desire for profit to a necessity for a perfect form of currency. The impending revolution is the recognition that the current monetary system is flawed, and all financialized wealth will eventually find its way into the secure embrace of Bitcoin, a flawless reserve asset.

A simple concept which just requires a modicum of faith in a reserve replacement of the current full faith and credit forced down our throats by guns and laws in this broken money system. That faith is not unfounded as Bitcoin has been unsuccessfully attacked by the very system it intends to fix, hundreds of times.

Bitcoin can run easily in parallel to dollars; but its presence will inevitably illuminate the shortcomings of the current system.

Bitcoin does not demand blind faith, but rather invites you to consider the possibility of a paradigm shift, a crack in the wall of your normalcy bias. It offers an alternative to the broken system we wake up to each day, a system that we may not even realize is flawed.

The reason we "go down the rabbit hole" is that Bitcoin carries a spiritual component; truth. Truth by math. People are generally repelled by truth. I know this because, when I am bothered by someone I prefer not to talk to within social settings, I mention the topic of Bitcoin, and they miraculously vanish. Bitcoin is both compelling and repelling simultaneously. Just who will be blessed by Bitcoin? Bitcoin will be tender and gentle, and run parallel to dollars until dollars virally vanish. You might be thinking nonsense! I suggest you keep reading.

The Bitcoin Design Works

Bitcoin works flawlessly every time.

Bitcoin will dematerialize every asset that can be financially represented, every stock, and every square inch of real estate, bonds, gold, literature, artwork, song, and everything by placing it on the blockchain.

This value will be stored and efficiently dispensed at the owner's slightest wish at the speed of light. All this is in an entirely and instantly verifiable state. This will revolutionize the credit world and give banks a new mission of integrity rather than corruption and obfuscation. Banks' new master will become the consensus of the people rather than the FED.

I will not belabor the Bitcoin gainsayer but to say they exist. These disputers usually have an intense connection to the dollar and use it to further their modus operandi. Butt kissing types.

There are certain people such as Peter Schiff (a Bitcoin gainsayer) who, by the way, I admire for his leaning towards Austrian economics (basically money with little inflation). I have listened to him over the years and agree that physical gold is a superior value proposition to fiat. Schiff's argument for gold was done with a backdrop of fiat dollars. He sells gold to the public by accepting dollars in exchange, which he rails against. I suspect that Peter Schiff's father's fight against the IRS, which took his life in jail, created a solid link to the dollar/gold argument, not the dollar/Bitcoin argument. Shout out to Peter. Make the argument dollar vs. Bitcoin. In memory of your faithful father, forget gold for five minutes. Bitcoin vs. dollars is the honest debate.

Get Out of Dollars ASAP

Acknowledge that dollars are money by decree, a flawed fiat system. Whereas Bitcoin is money by willing consensus. Each and everyone's individual and collective faith that makes it work well.

We're still in the early stages, but a seismic shift is on the horizon. The experts, the *institutional money*, are cornered and forced to acknowledge Bitcoin's potential. Even though they're deeply rooted in the dollar system, they can't ignore the immense opportunity Bitcoin presents. The genie is about to be released from the bottle, and it's an exciting time to be part of this change.

Consider the debates you have heard. The discussion never addresses how dollars are nothing based on nothing and worth even less, and yet only work because of the tremendous need for money, even if it is severely flawed;

a vacuum cannot be tolerated. Peter Schiff's argument is that Bitcoin is nothing. Yet it has the largest decentralized network, securing it through proof-of-work and verifying the distributed ledger day in and day out. What do dollars have, proof-of-work?   No An immutable decentralized ledger that is perfect in every jot-and-tittle? No. Let the debate compare dollars to Bitcoin. HELLO! I say, what is a bank or brokerage statement if not numbers on a questionable ledger? Does anyone recall Bernie Madoff? Or can anyone say bank bailout; Silicon Valley Bank (SVB), perhaps, or any of dozens of belly-up, bailed-out banks in the last year? Can confidence and conviction be applied to "laughing all the way to the bank" any longer? The US Treasury has convinced us to do bailouts of their friends through the magical inflation mechanism. They have made provision to bail-out these select banks on the backs of every dollar holder not the taxpayer, as you have been swindled into believing.

Peter Schiff, once a hero, is sadly becoming irrelevant as Bitcoin grows larger every year. The Bitcoin mechanism cannot be defeated.

21 Million Vs.

My First Steps

My journey with Bitcoin began in Dec of 2011. At first, I thought it intriguing but dismissed it without much thought. My gainsaying phase. This concept kept me awake and continued to roll around in my mind. I wanted to learn more, so on a whim, I ordered a Jalapeño Bitcoin miner a few months later.   It took nine months to arrive. When my baby arrived, I started Bitcoin mining. With a little research, I saw the unit had been mining well before I received it, for about ten months, prior to my order. Yes, a scam which I had been noticing with pre ordered mining equipment. Long story short, time was (extreme money) along that particular Bitcoin timeline.   Presumably manufactures were skimming; and no guarantee was provided for definitive delivery; also mining contracts were being perfected along those lines to skim time profit from those rigs.

Bitcoin is a nascent asset class. Actually, I would denote Bitcoin as an official asset class upon the ETF approval; which is only weeks from an assured green light. This would act as an onramp for those unfamiliar with the power and security of holding the underlying asset. Still this asset class will out shine any and all that have come before it. This is the surest and easiest money to be made for years to come. In 2023, Bitcoin rose 160%, give or take, as the year isn't over yet; and it is approaching a trillion dollar market capitalization. This leaves a lot of room to absorb a worldwide 700 trillion dollar market.

Beyond that, in a world free of financial corruption and terminated inflation, productivity is bound to rise to the stars, and 700 trillion might rise higher by orders of magnitude. So will Bitcoin.

Cognitive Dissonance

 Cognitive dissonance is the seeing but not believing. The definition is having inconsistent thoughts, beliefs, or attitudes, especially relating to behavioral decisions. This is the mass viewpoint currently attached to Bitcoin.

Let's take the Bitcoin price history from the past to the present and then project it into the future using the past as a guide to future price. This way, we will be able to define the ebb and flow of cognitive dissonance until there is a new criterion of a Bitcoin normalcy bias.

We will all get Bitcoin, but not all at the same price.

Bitcoin is Analogous to Things of Order

The gradual shift from traditional fiat currencies, such as the U.S. dollar to Bitcoin, represents a transformative trend in the global financial landscape. Initially, individuals and institutions will engage in a slow and cautious exploration of the decentralized digital currency, testing its waters as a potential store of value and medium of exchange. Increasing awareness, growing business acceptance, and a desire for financial autonomy, will contribute to this steady migration. However, the real watershed moment might occur suddenly, catalyzed by a confluence of events, such as economic uncertainties, currency devaluations, or systemic crises that carry on endlessly. A palpable tipping point will prompt a mass realization of Bitcoin's resilience and its potential to serve as an answer to traditional financial vulnerabilities. As confidence in the conventional financial system wanes, the masses will pivot swiftly towards Bitcoin, seeking refuge in its inflation-proof nature. This rapid and widespread adoption will signify a paradigm shift, underscoring Bitcoin's emergence as a cornerstone in the future of global finance. In reality, Bitcoin is not a hedge, but an answer to all problems with money.

Hyperinflation Can Happen to Dollars but not Bitcoin

High inflation and hyperinflation are phenomena that can occur when a country experiences an extreme and rapid increase in the supply of its currency, leading to a sharp devaluation of its purchasing power. The fundamental difference between the U.S. dollar and Bitcoin lies in their respective monetary policies. The U.S. dollar is subject to the discretion of central banks and governments, which can and will print more dollars, fueling, then sparking, and finally, fanning inflation. In contrast, Bitcoin operates on a fixed and decentralized supply configuration. With a capped supply of 21 million coins, Bitcoin is designed specifically to be immune to inflationary pressures. The decentralized nature of Bitcoin, secured by blockchain technology, ensures that no single entity can manipulate its supply. As a result, Bitcoin offers a solution against any high or hyperinflationary risks that are directly associated with traditional fiat currencies. This makes Bitcoin an attractive alternative for those seeking a store of value at any time, especially now. Don't get caught holding the fiat bag.

Verifying Gold and Silvers Authenticity

Verifying the authenticity of gold and silver involves sophisticated testing methods, such as assaying, spectroscopy, or physical examination by experts. These methods confirm the relative purity of the precious metals. Conversely, Bitcoin's pure authenticity is verified through its blockchain, a transparent and immutable ledger that records each and every transaction in the network. Each Bitcoin transaction is verified by a consensus mechanism among network participants, completely eliminating any need for a central authority. In the physical realm, gold and silver's authenticity relies on tangible characteristics, while Bitcoin's authenticity is rooted in cryptographic math and a distributed consensus. The comparison underscores the evolution from traditional, tangible assets to digital, decentralized assets. Both gold, silver, and Bitcoin offer distinct advantages, with the former rooted in physical properties and the latter, in the secure and transparent nature of the Bitcoin blockchain technology; the bottom line is that Bitcoin can unquestionably and simply be authenticated by anyone, anywhere, anytime on **https://www.blockchain.com/explorer** in an instant.

Bitcoin is a Store of Value or Reserve Currency

Bitcoin's role in the financial landscape has evolved beyond being merely a conventional currency; instead, it has emerged as a nascent, yet prominent store of value and a potential reserve currency. While traditional currencies, like the U.S. dollar or euro, primarily function as mediums of exchange for daily transactions, Bitcoin distinguishes itself by serving as a decentralized and finite digital asset. Its capped supply of 21 million coins naturally positions it as a robust store of value. Investors and institutions increasingly view Bitcoin as the final answer to inflation and economic uncertainties, a role traditionally played by gold. Furthermore, the term "reserve currency" suggests that Bitcoin will be held by central banks and individuals as a stable and reliable asset. As its adoption grows and its characteristics as a store of value become more pronounced, Bitcoin is carving out a unique space in the global financial landscape, challenging conventional notions of what constitutes money.

Advantages of Bitcoin

Bitcoin proudly illustrates many advantages contributing to its growth and prominence in the financial world. First and foremost, Bitcoin operates on a peer-to-peer network that completely eliminates the need for intermediaries like banks. The fixed supply of 21 million coins ensures scarcity, providing an answer to eliminate inflation, which in reality is the largest and most hidden and surreptitious of taxes. Bitcoin transactions are transparent and recorded on an immutable blockchain, enhancing security and eliminating the risk of fraud on layer one. Its global accessibility allows anyone with an Internet connection to independently participate, promoting financial inclusion. Bitcoin transactions are pseudonymous, offering a substantial degree of privacy. As a borderless digital asset, it facilitates international transactions without needing currency conversions or traditional banking systems, making it a practical solution for cross-border payments. The permission-less nature of Bitcoin means anyone can participate in its network without requiring approval. Additionally, the decentralized consensus mechanism, known as proof-of-work, adds robustness to its security. These combined advantages position Bitcoin as a resilient and innovative financial instrument, garnering interest and adoption worldwide; further, deletions of inefficiencies such as foreign currency conversions and bank fees here at home and many other frictions of cash dollars grease the skids for adoption.

The Expanding Network

The expanding network of Bitcoin is a critical element of enhancing its value proposition. As the Bitcoin network grows, more participants contribute to its security. The increasing number of nodes, miners, and users reinforces the network's resilience, making it more resistant to attacks and censorship. The distributed nature of the network ensures that no single entity can control or manipulate Bitcoin, instilling trust and reliability. Moreover, the growing user base and adoption by businesses contribute to Bitcoin's liquidity, making it more viable as a medium of exchange. The expanding network not only bolsters the security and reliability of Bitcoin but is a self-fulfilling prophecy as it solidifies its position as a transformative force in the world of finance. When considering the contrast between dollars or any fiat-based asset in the world today, Bitcoin is light-years ahead of the rest in terms of almost every aspect of what money should be. Given this, Bitcoin will naturally rise quickly to the top of the financial food chain. I believe there is a very small chance that manipulators **MAY** already realize this, and any further resistance may just be a red herring to allow the system time to back up the truck. This is one deep rabbit hole.

Leading Investment

Bitcoin resonates with investors seeking alternatives to traditional financial systems.   The transparent and immutable nature of the blockchain technology provides a robust foundation for trust, eliminating the risk of fraud and manipulation in the Bitcoin mechanism. But the war against Bitcoin will rage on unsuccessfully, initiated by a dollar system now struggling for air. Bitcoin's increasing acceptance by institutional investors, coupled with its global accessibility, enhances its liquidity and market depth, making it a viable investment option for all individuals and business entities. Young children today will not know what banks are tomorrow. The historical performance of Bitcoin, a staggering 5 billion percent increase, in a scant 14 years. This is a most impressive price appreciation, attracting attention and confidence to its long-term value. All this on top of the fact that it works perfectly every transaction for trillions of transactions. As a result, Bitcoin's unique combination of scarcity, decentralization, transparency, and adoption positions it as a leading and compelling investment.

Shitcoin Movement

$$$ Investments in "shitcoins," a colloquial term often used to describe thousands of low-quality or speculative cryptocurrencies with questionable fundamentals, will shift towards the asset Bitcoin over time. While the cryptocurrency market is diverse, with numerous projects and tokens, most lack the robustness, security, and widespread recognition that Bitcoin enjoys. As an example, Solana keeps doing airdrops to stimulate the network with freebies, thereby showing exaggerated network usage. This network exaggeration sucks in buyers; as a result, this is a fabricated shitcoin economy. These economies are typically a flash in the pan. As investors gain experience and seek more established assets, they often gravitate toward Bitcoin as the flagship. The movement of investments from "shitcoins" to Bitcoin reflects a broader trend toward increased market maturity, and the recognition of Bitcoin as a reliable and resilient digital asset.

Spot ETF

The eventual unveiling of a spot Bitcoin exchange-traded fund (ETF) holds earth-shaking potential, impacting the price of Bitcoin. It will start with a trickle and finish with a tsunami. Currently, we are in the trickle phase. A spot Bitcoin ETF will provide institutional and retail investors with a regulated and accessible avenue to gain quick exposure to the tracked asset without understanding Bitcoin at all. It is also better than other derivative products that do not require Bitcoin to be attached to it. The spot ETF is NOT the Bitcoin asset itself but an index of Bitcoin. An eggroll wrapper only. One whereby the filling (Bitcoin) you will never get to touch, much less taste. This means you shall not taste the fruits of the underlying asset: FREEDOM.

This development anticipates attracting substantial capital from traditional financial markets into Bitcoin, subsequently driving up the price of Bitcoin. The ETF's introduction could also serve as a signal of mainstream acceptance and perceived regulatory clarity, seemingly alleviating concerns related to market manipulation and security. The Bitcoin spot ETF is **only an indexed product** to Bitcoin, not Bitcoin itself. However, the ETF carries weight as it requires actual Bitcoin to have a one-to-one relationship with the ETF. As seen with other financial assets, the creation of ETFs has historically correlated with strongly increased demand. In the case of Bitcoin, this will lead to an extraordinary surge in investor confidence and interest. I approve of this "on-ramp," but caution investors to quickly get educated and move any gains made from the ETF into the underlying asset for a myriad of reasons later expounded upon.

Lost or Destroyed Bitcoin Will Never be Recovered

$$$ The exact number of lost or destroyed Bitcoins is difficult to ascertain. Still, it is estimated that a significant portion of the total Bitcoin supply is inaccessible due to lost private keys or hardware failures. Early in Bitcoin's history, when its value was relatively low, users treated their Bitcoins as less than cherished, resulting in losing or neglecting access to private keys. Moreover, with the increased use of early mining equipment and now-obsolete storage methods, some Bitcoins are unrecoverable. While specific figures vary, estimates suggest that a substantial number of up to 25% of Bitcoins have been lost, and these "zombie coins" will likely never be recovered, reducing the effective circulating supply. This scarcity contributes to the deflationary nature of Bitcoin, with the lost coins serving as a unique aspect of its economic model and adding to the overall narrative of digital scarcity. Each lost Bitcoin is then distributed across

the complete Bitcoin ecosphere, laterally benefiting each of the holders of Bitcoin in circulation, with an equal share relative to Bitcoins owned automatically. This would be inflation in reverse. It is a sporadic phenomenon indeed. Bitcoin owners will not realize this value immediately, but only when adoptions mature.

Gary Gensler's Stance

Gary Gensler serves as the U.S. Securities and Exchange Commission (SEC) Chairman. He was sworn in as the SEC Chairman in April 2021. Gensler has a background in both public service and academia, including his previous role as the Commodity Futures Trading Commission (CFTC) Chairman. His stance on Bitcoin is characterized by a commitment to regulatory oversight and his professed investor protection. I think he is acting more like a political animal rather than the legal administrator he was placed there to be. I don't have much good to convey in regards to Mr. Gary Gensler. In my personal opinion, he will not be long-lived in his current role as SEC chair anyway, losing two major federal cases against the Bitcoin ETF and Ripple. I don't believe Gary Gensler will fight the court's decision on the Bitcoin spot ETF. This confluence of events ending with an approved ETF will open a Pandora's Box of nightmares for bureaucrats everywhere. It was an inevitable blessing to chip away at the despots' power grab. It will not end easily or pretty, either. Bitcoin will thrive as a result of the coming ETF.

Actually, the longer he remains in his seat at the SEC, the more I believe the system has surreptitiously embraced Bitcoin. What a crazy world.

A Tool of Empowerment

Bitcoin serves as a powerful tool of empowerment by providing individuals with financial autonomy. Its decentralized nature, operating on a peer-to-peer network, allows users to transact without the need for intermediaries. This is particularly impactful in regions with limited access to traditional banking services, empowering the unbanked or underbanked populations to participate in the global economy. Bitcoin's borderless nature facilitates cross-border transactions without constraints, offering a financial lifeline to those in areas with restrictive banking infrastructure. Additionally, Bitcoin answers inflation and economic uncertainties, allowing individuals to preserve their wealth from termites such as inflation. The ownership of private keys gives users complete control over their funds, enhancing security and eliminating the risk of asset seizure if properly stored. Overall, Bitcoin empowers individuals by providing financial freedom and a means to protect and grow their wealth independently of traditional economic structures.

Bitcoin Halving

$$$ The Bitcoin halving is a programmed event that occurs approximately every four years, reducing the reward miners receive for validating transactions by half, often triggering a supply shock. This mechanism is designed to cut the natural supply of new Bitcoins in half until no more rewards exist. The typical impact on the price of Bitcoin is rooted in the principles of supply and demand. As the rate of new supply entering the market decreases during a halving, and demand remains constant or increases, the scarcity of Bitcoins drives up their value. Historical patterns suggest that previous halving events have been correlated with significant price rallies for Bitcoin. The anticipation of reduced natural supply coupled with the growing recognition of Bitcoin as a store of value, tends to attract investors' attention. It is not a stagnant store of value, but rather a fruit-bearing asset, year in and year out.

Bitcoin HODLers

The exact number of Bitcoin HODLers, a term coined within the Bitcoin community referring to long-term holders who resist selling despite market fluctuations, is difficult to number due to the pseudonymous nature of Bitcoin transactions. However, various blockchain analytics tools attempt to estimate the number of addresses associated with long-term holdings. It is suggested that an all-time high of 71% of Bitcoin holders, or HODLers as they are known, haven't moved any Bitcoin in more than a year. This number is steadily growing, indicating a trend toward a trusted flight to safety and an understanding of the Bitcoin value proposition.

The behavior of long-term investors, "HODLers," is closely watched. Their commitment to holding onto their investments through various market cycles is seen as a measure of underlying confidence in the asset's future. Related Bitcoin Price Analysis for November 30th 2023: While short-term traders often react to immediate price movements and news, the steady accumulation by long-term investors points to a collective expectation of future gains. This matches the expanding HODLers chart. The implication of this for the Bitcoin market is immense. A high HODLer balance typically indicates a further reduction in offers to sell, which could lay the groundwork for a future unlimited bullish phase. More on this later....

Pricing Mechanisms of Bitcoin

The spot price of Bitcoin referred to simply as the current market price, is determined by the interaction of buyers and sellers on various cryptocurrency exchanges.

Supply and demand: Like any asset, the spot price of Bitcoin is strongly influenced by the basic economic principles of supply and demand.

Higher liquidity, characterized by a more significant number of buyers and sellers, tends to result in more stable pricing. Market sentiment and external news factors, regulatory developments, macroeconomic trends, and market sentiment can significantly impact the spot price. Positive news often leads to increased demand and higher prices, while negative news can result in a decrease in demand and lower prices.

It's important to note that, unlike the stock market, the Bitcoin market operates 24/7/365 days every year, and the decentralized and global nature of Bitcoin means that it is traded on numerous exchanges all over the world, contributing to a diverse and dynamic pricing environment.

Meanwhile, stocks and bonds and other various Wall Street issues, comparatively, are only traded 19% of the time, contrasted to Bitcoin. Bitcoin is a truly open marketplace.

Underdeveloped Countries

$$$ The adoption of Bitcoin in underdeveloped countries and among the underbanked population is already underway. The pace of awareness and usage is expected

to continue growing exponentially. Bitcoin presents significant opportunities for individuals in such regions. Financial inclusion in areas with limited access to traditional banking services covers most of the world. Bitcoin offers an accessible financial system. People can now participate in the global economy without bending a knee to traditional banking infrastructure. Before now, let's face it, they never would have been banked or had a chance to prosper.

Bitcoin can provide a more cost-effective and efficient way for people in underdeveloped countries to receive remittances from family members working abroad. It eliminates the need for intermediaries and fiat-related transaction costs.

In countries experiencing high inflation or economic instability, which can be unwieldy, Bitcoin's finite supply makes it an attractive option as a store of value and an answer to currency depreciation.

They now have access to investment opportunities. Bitcoin allows individuals in underdeveloped regions to invest in land and access global financial markets, opening up possibilities that would be impossible through traditional investment channels.

Bitcoin enables micro-transactions through layer two Lightning Network or other network protocols. This can be particularly beneficial in regions where access to capital is limited.

While the benefits are apparent, as awareness grows and technological infrastructure improves, more people in underdeveloped countries will likely explore and adopt Bitcoin even more quickly. Moreover, initiatives and projects focused on educating communities about Bitcoin and blockchain technology, along with the development of user-friendly wallets and interfaces, are playing a role in facilitating adoption. In summary, as the broader Bitcoin ecosystem matures, it has the potential to offer inclusive financial solutions to those who have been underserved by banks.

BlackRock is Buying Mining Capacity

It's important to note that the Bitcoin market, including Bitcoin mining, has seen increased institutional interest due to the potential for returns and the growing recognition of digital assets as a legitimate investment class. Some institutional investors view Bitcoin mining operations as a wholesale way to gain exposure to the cryptocurrency market and benefit from its long-term growth.

If BlackRock, or any other entity, is actively acquiring mining capacity, it could be driven by a range of factors; such as the belief in the long-term viability of Bitcoin, a desire to diversify investment portfolios, or an interest in participating in the underlying infrastructure of blockchain networks which support Bitcoin. Be assured that BlackRock is actively acquiring mining capacity. And Fidelity has been mining Bitcoin quietly since 2010. For you *Doctor Strangelove* fans out there, we are talking "precious bodily fluids."

The Dollar is a Failing Currency

Describing the U.S. dollar as a "failing" currency is a subjective assessment. However, some critics and analysts express concerns about certain aspects of the U.S. dollar and the broader monetary system. Commonly raised in discussions about the potential challenges facing the U.S. dollar are: Have we printed enough money? Can we print some more? Can we change the name of printing vast amounts of cash to quantitative easing?

Critics argue that the U.S. Federal Reserve's monetary policies, including low-interest rates and quantitative easing, may lead to inflationary pressures, eroding the dollar's purchasing power over time.

The United States has accumulated a substantial national debt, and many worry about the sustainability of such high debt levels. A growing debt burden will affect confidence in the U.S. dollar, especially if there are concerns about the government's inability to manage debt. No one seems to flinch anymore when 3 trillion is added overnight.

The U.S. dollar serves as the world's primary reserve currency, but there are debates about the potential challenges to its dominance. Some countries and entities seek alternatives or diversification away from the dollar.

Political and geopolitical events can impact the strength of a currency. Trade tensions, sanctions, and international conflicts can contribute to uncertainties that affect the value of the U.S. dollar.

Talk about your walking dead.

The rise of digital currencies and the emergence of other currencies, including central bank digital currencies (CBDCs) and private cryptocurrencies, has sparked discussions about the future role of traditional fiat currencies, including the U.S. dollar. The Internet has provided rise to different digital payment systems with varying accessibility, privacy, settlement, and governance. Now, the U.S. is considering proposals for its own "digital dollar;" as digital money plays a quickly increasing and significant role in our lives.

Currently, the U.S. dollar remains a widely used and accepted medium of exchange globally. However, discussions around the future of currencies, including the potential for new forms of digital or alternative currencies, proliferate. Investors and policymakers closely monitor these factors as part of a broader assessment of the global financial landscape.

Bitcoin Stocks and Bonds

Bitcoin operates on a decentralized network using mining. New Bitcoins are created to reward miners who contribute computing power to secure the network and validate transactions. The open source issuance is algorithmically controlled in a sharply diminishing fashion, making it a stable asset.

Stocks represent ownership in a company, and new shares are typically issued through corporate actions like initial public offerings (IPOs) or secondary offerings. On the other hand, bonds represent debt, and new issuances occur when entities, including governments and corporations, borrow money from investors. If you prefer not to mine Bitcoin, it can be purchased using a cryptocurrency exchange. Most people will be unable to purchase an entire BTC because of its price, but you can buy **fractions** of BTC on exchanges with fiat currency.

Fixed Supply vs. Variable Issuance

The total supply of Bitcoin is hard capped at 21 million, and the issuance rate is reduced through a halving that occurs approximately every four years. This fixed supply contrasts with fiat currencies, where central banks can print more money at will and with abandon.

Stocks and Bonds: The supply of stocks can increase over time due to new issuances. Bonds are a terrible debt investment proposition almost always outpaced by inflation alone.

Market dynamics of Bitcoin, which operates constantly in an uninterrupted global market without centralized, or for that matter, corrupt control. Its value is determined by supply and demand dynamics, influenced predominantly by factors such as relative adoption, investor sentiment, and macroeconomic conditions.

Stocks and Bonds are traded on stock exchanges with specific trading hours, excluding holidays and long weekends, regular weekends, circuit breakers, and COVID-19; you get the gist. Prices are influenced by company performance, economic indicators, and market sentiment, such as front running or paint the tape and high-frequency trading.

Bitcoin is highly divisible, with the smallest unit being a Satoshi (0.00000001) Bitcoin, allowing for micro-transactions. When a Bitcoin equals 1 million dollars, a SAT or Satoshi will equal 1¢ a penny.

While stocks are typically indivisible, bonds can be traded in fractional units. However, certain securities may have restrictions and minimum purchase requirements.

Bitcoin's supply is algorithmically controlled and capped, offering a unique model compared to the issuance of stocks and bonds, which involves centralized authorities and dilutive dynamics influenced by corporate "decisions." Stocks and bonds are dollar-denominated.

Governments Create Volatility

The government has a strong motive to actively seek to create volatility in Bitcoin to protect the dollar. Bitcoin's price volatility is primarily driven by governments and regulatory bodies, which are exploring ways to regulate and manage the impact of Bitcoin on dollars. Bitcoin is considered a disruptive currency to all freely printed fiat. An avenue exists for deliberate government actions. One scenario might be for the government or its relationship with the FED (Federal Reserve) to allocate (print) dollars to purchase Bitcoin in such a way as to drive the price very high. This would create a buzz and the market would FOMO, then shortly thereafter dump Bitcoin while taking full advantage of the short position, and make a tidy profit in the process. This is conjecture surrounding blood-sucking tics in general. The result is a convincing argument that manipulators have created and managed volatility. Many potential market participants would naturally shy away. The manipulators will wait until it is ripe to do it again. I say don't worry, be happy. Just HODL like your life depends on it. Better yet, dollar cost average. Despite the unnatural volatility, ask yourself why Bitcoin keeps going higher, despite this volatility. Keep on asking that question, *hopefully* after you have secured a position.

FOMO

"FOMO" stands for "Fear of Missing Out." It is a psychological phenomenon where individuals experience anxiety or uneasiness, driven by the perception that others are participating in a rewarding experience or investment opportunity from which they are absent. In the context of financial markets, including Bitcoin assets, FOMO often refers to the fear of missing out on potential profits when an asset's price is rapidly rising. This is a common occurrence with Bitcoin. The only thing you can do is educate yourself and buy all you can afford, then buy more when it is higher, kicking yourself all along the way to your next "*why didn't I buy more earlier*" purchase. There are a lot of you out there who know exactly what I am talking about!

$$$ When a particular investment, such as Bitcoin, experiences a sudden surge in price or shows signs of significant upward momentum, individuals who were initially hesitant may be tempted to join the trend out of fear that they will miss out on promising gains. This fear can lead to impulsive buying decisions, contributing to further price increases.

FOMO is a powerful emotional driver in markets and can result in irrational behavior, as investors may disregard fundamental analysis and succumb to the pressure of not wanting to miss out on budding opportunities. This may be a lucky stroke for some, but the same FOMO can succumb to FUD (fear, uncertainty, doubt) without education or reading this book. It's essential for investors to approach markets with a rational and well-informed mindset, considering the risks and fundamentals rather than being solely driven by the fear of missing out. Undoubtedly, FOMO has led to incredible gains for some. Still, since their profits were predicated on emotion, they invariably sell at an inopportune time; and also miss the much more significant gain they would have had; if only they HODLed like Ron Popeil's "set it and forget it" mantra.

Where Will New Inflows Come?

$$$ The future sources of new inflows into Bitcoin will come from new and various sectors and entities as the Bitcoin ecosystem continues to evolve. Some potential sources, like the involvement of institutional investors, have just started unfolding, with hedge funds, family offices, and corporations allocating funds to Bitcoin as a store of value. Bitcoin will become a new asset class when the ETF is approved. There will be a multiplier impact associated with the passage of the ETF. Confidence will emerge over the next year and decade. As commercials play repeatedly, Bitcoin will be in your face and ubiquitous. This will cause continued institutional adoption and will bring substantial inflows into the market, which will cause

an endless feedback loop: retail feeds institutional, feeds more commercials, feeds a ubiquitous trend, and feeds institutions, completes the never ending cycle loop. Many investment management firms have indicated up to 6% recommended allocation into the ETF right from the starting post. This is as big as most new asset classes, such as the gold ETF, which was recommended at 1% initially, and grew to 6%. I suspect that 20% or 25% is not out of the question with this asset class.

Retail investors, including individuals and small-scale investors, are likely to continue contributing to Bitcoin's growth. As awareness increases, user-friendly platforms make it easier for people to buy and hold Bitcoin.

$$$ Following the trend set by companies like MicroStrategy and Tesla, more corporations are considering allocating part of their treasury reserves to Bitcoin as a store of value.

$$$ Decentralized finance (DeFi) continues to gain traction; users are seeking exposure to Bitcoin through decentralized exchanges and lending platforms, contributing to increased liquidity and capital flows.

$$$ In Emerging Markets regions with economic instability, high inflation, or restricted access to traditional financial services, individuals are turning to Bitcoin to preserve wealth and access global financial markets.

$$$ Innovation and Financial Product development begets new financial products and investment vehicles, such as

Bitcoin exchange-traded funds (ETFs) or other structured products. They are attracting capital from traditional investors seeking regulated exposure to Bitcoin.

$$$ Government and Central Bank Adoption is gaining significant traction. Some countries and central banks are using Bitcoin as the dominos keep falling. If governments or central banks decide to hold or invest in Bitcoin, it could represent a *"beyond massive"* source of new inflows.

$$$ Additionally, advancements in blockchain technology and scalability solutions will undoubtedly lead to increased adoption and confidence in Bitcoin, attracting new participants who may have been hesitant due to concerns about transaction speed and fees, and they will capitulate. It would be impossible to identify and determine all the sources and magnitude of future inflows into Bitcoin, but isn't it fun to try, especially if you have a position?

Currently the state of gut is a nervous condition, leaving most helplessly unable to cope with the state of financial affairs. New inflows may grow from this. Initially, Bitcoin attracted idea investors and then speculators, but now, as Bitcoin enters a safe and proven asset class, the nervous condition will move old assets to the new Bitcoin. Yes, FOMO will still be a factor, possibly to a greater extent. But my point is that with education, Bitcoin will grow from the enlarged debasement of all fiat currencies.

What is DeFi

DeFi stands for Decentralized Finance, which refers to a set of financial services and applications built on blockchain technology. The core idea behind DeFi is to recreate traditional financial systems, such as banking, lending, and trading, in a decentralized and open-source manner, removing the need for traditional intermediaries like banks and brokers.

Key components and features of the DeFi ecosystem include smart contracts. DeFi applications are typically built on blockchain platforms that support smart contracts. Smart contracts are self-executing agreements with the terms of the contract directly written into code. Decentralized exchanges are platforms that enable users to trade various cryptocurrencies directly with one another, without the need for an intermediary. Users retain control of their private keys and funds throughout the trading process.

Decentralized Autonomous Organizations (DAOs): DAOs are entities represented by rules encoded as a computer program that is transparent, controlled by the organization members, and not influenced by a central government. In DeFi, DAOs are often used for governance and decision-making.

DeFi applications require real-world data to function effectively and efficiently. Oracles act as bridges between blockchain networks and the real world, providing accurate and timely information such as prices, data, etc. DeFi has gained significant attention for its potential to democratize finance, increase financial inclusion, and provide more accessible and transparent financial services. However, it's important to note that the DeFi space is still relatively young but growing exponentially.

DeFi is subject to risks and market volatility.

Number of Bitcoin Actively Traded on Exchanges

$$$ According to Bitcoin metrics at the time of this writing, less than 1.8 million Bitcoin, is a very thin inventory in the order book. This, especially in light of the fact that a spot ETF will absorb most Bitcoins in a matter of months. This is an ever-thinning herd. Such will undoubtedly boost the price to soaring heights. Additionally, an all-time high of over 71% of HODLers' coins have not moved in the last year and are tightening supply even more. These HODLers are growing in size.

Gresham's law is an economic principle that states, "Bad money drives out good." This principle prescribes that if there are two forms of money in circulation, Bitcoin and dollars, people will tend to hoard the money they consider to be of higher value (good money) and use the money they consider to be of lower value (lousy money) for transactions. The reasoning behind this behavior is that people will seek to get rid of the lower-value money first, keeping the higher-value money for themselves. This is what is occurring with gold, silver, and Bitcoin. Over time, the lower-value money circulates more widely, while the higher-value money is hoarded or used in other ways, such as a reserve asset or commodity. This phenomenon can lead to the disappearance of the higher-value money from circulation. This, as you will see, is the thesis of this book, "Bitcoin's Violent Upside." The market for Bitcoin will still exist, but trying to buy some will soon be the real challenge, and at what enormous price can I obtain any?

When I was a young shaver, my granddad would offer me two dimes in exchange for every pure silver one I found in my change. I thought he was non-compos mentis and started losing it. But the entrepreneur that I was, would go to the bank and buy a roll of dimes, sort them, and invariably find five or six silver out of the lot. This expanded to sorting many rolls of dimes and quarters. And weekly, I would make a tidy profit. Today, pure silver coinage is all but gone; it's Gresham's law. By the way, the old codger was clever as a fox, because silver dimes are worth fifteen times what a regular dime is worth today. This is happening with Bitcoin today, and soon, they will not be found in circulation *except* at a much higher price.

The Fed "Prints" Dollars to Try and Save the System

The Federal Reserve, as the central bank of the United States, has the authority to modify and lever the money supply and implement monetary policy. While the phrase "printing more dollars" is a simplification, the Federal Reserve has dominion over the money supply, and it often takes actions to "manage" economic stability. The Fed buys or sells government securities on the open market to control the federal funds rate and bear upon the money supply. It is not as complicated as they would like you to think. In essence, money printer go Brrrrrrrrrrrrrrrrr.

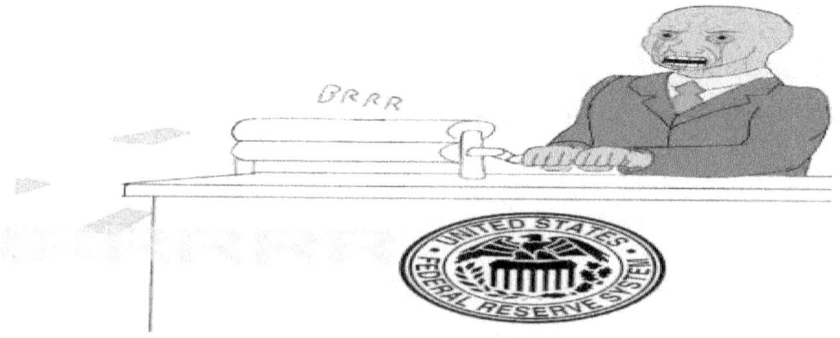

QE

The Fed sets the discount rate, which is the interest rate at which banks can borrow directly from the central bank. Changes in the discount rate impact borrowing and lending throughout the banking system.

The Fed can tweak the credit by loosening or contracting, much like in the Great Depression. The FED has advanced knowledge of this tweaking. We pawns do not.

$$$ In times of economic stress, the Fed may engage in QE (Quantitative Easing), where it buys financial assets, typically government securities, to increase the money supply and lower long-term interest rates. This kind of gives the word "counterfeiting" a whole new meaning. This is to maintain maximum employment and stable prices ostensibly. You be the judge.

Wait for it.... Wait for it.... The Pivot.

The effectiveness and consequences of these monetary policies are the subject of ongoing debate among economists and policymakers. Not so much, we the pawns. Better said in the parlance of Sargent Shultz, "I know nothing."

Mental Inflation

"Mental inflation" is an informal economic term that could describe a psychological phenomenon related to people's perceptions of prices and economic conditions.

Actual inflation, it is thought, refers to the general increase in the prices of goods and services over time. This is the most enormous monetary lie you were ever to learn. It is right up there with Santa Claus; the only difference is that you believe in inflation to this very day.

The FED will tell you inflation is a multifaceted phenomenon influenced by various economic, structural, and psychological factors. If you learn nothing else from this book, understand this: printing money is inflation.

Printing Money IS Inflation

Printing is not the cause of inflation; printing money IS inflation, and the FED is printing a lot of it. No, thank you, Jerome Powel. I did not order 300 Lbs. of meadow muffins. The FED would have you believe that they are trying to control inflation when, in fact, they are the originator and provider of inflation. The FED has only two choices: Let the debt collapse or print. Print it is! This is the most significant way they steal money from you—day in and day out. The FED would have you believe that your wealth is dissipating on its own; and you have no other choice except to work harder to stem the receding tide. Bitcoin is the only way to plug the holes in your bag.

I tell you here and now that Bitcoin has zero leaks.

The SEC is Attempting to Rule by Force

Rather than providing a crypto framework of rules, a combination of velvet ropes and force is cheaper and seemingly more effective.

The SEC's purported role is to protect investors and maintain fair and efficient markets. When it comes to Bitcoin specifically and cryptocurrencies in general, the SEC has taken various measures to scare the market when convenient. All of this depends on their puppet masters, who rhyme with Slack Rock, a large investment management firm. When the SEC is asked to drag their feet, they drag their feet. They produce evil villains from the Mt.Gox story and the FTX story, to keep the Bitcoin price down until the big boys can back up the truck. (((Just my opinion))) don't shoot this messenger. I promise not to point further accusatory fingers.

The SEC has taken enforcement actions, including legal action against certain initial coin offerings (ICOs) and token issuers, proclaiming them to violate securities laws; outside of the USA??? This is done to address cases where digital assets are considered securities, and their issuance or trading falls under existing regulatory frameworks. FYI, Bitcoin **cannot** be considered a security! Mainly because there is no CEO of Bitcoin to put in jail. This means the threat of enforcement becomes unavailable to the long arm of the SEC.

The SEC model is to issue guidance to become regulation and then enshrined into law. Further, this requires the need for compliance with securities laws. Hence, "the job."

The SEC has engaged in dialogues with select industry participants to better understand the evolving cryptocurrency landscape. Roundtable discussions and public comments are avenues through which the SEC seeks input from the community, which it promptly discards; (((sorry, I did it again))).

While the SEC actively enforces existing regulations, there have been calls for more explicit and comprehensive REGULATORY FRAMEWORKS for cryptocurrencies. The cryptocurrency industry has evolved rapidly, and stakeholders, including the SEC, recognize the need for regulatory clarity to foster innovation while ensuring investor protections. This story goes down a deep, dark rabbit hole. One that is meant for my next book, maybe. Stay tuned.

Recent Enforcement Actions

Sam Bankman-Fried, the founder of the FTX cryptocurrency exchange, has been found guilty. All of his coworkers have pointed their fingers in an attempt to avoid jail time. I am unsure of anyone's guilt, but the vampires needed a fall guy and a continuous stream of fear surrounding Bitcoin to keep it down, and help banks get their footing in the lead-up to the spot ETF rollout. The same goes for customers who drained billions of dollars from Binance's crypto platform. Prosecutors are considering whether to file criminal charges against its founder and CEO, Changpeng Zhao, and other executives. Since its creation in 2017, the unit has brought over 80 enforcement actions related to fraudulent and unregistered crypto asset offerings and platforms, and this is just the back end. The front door was used to shelter campaign funds to well-known but nameless beneficiaries of Ukrainian funnels. Yet Bitcoin keeps rolling on. The SEC would love for you to believe that these platforms and exchanges are Bitcoin. **They are not!** Bitcoin and shitcoin cryptocurrencies are two separate entities. I keep them properly separated within this book, and you should also.

Bitcoin is a Budding Asset Class

$$$ Bitcoin is recognized as an emerging and distinct asset class. While the concept of Bitcoin as an asset class is still evolving, several factors contribute to its consideration as such. First and foremost, the spot Bitcoin ETF advances it to the head of the class. Bitcoin is often referred to as "digital gold" and is viewed correctly by investors as a strong store of value. Its limited supply, decentralized nature, and security features make it unique among traditional assets. *Decentralization* and *limited supply* is the heart of Bitcoin. Bitcoin operates on a blockchain, and its supply is capped at 21 million coins; I mention this often, hoping it becomes an inexorable law of nature within you, understanding scarcity like no other. It is these

characteristics which differentiate it from fiat currencies and other shitcoins.

Asymmetric Non-Correlating Asset

$$$ Bitcoin diversification is an asymmetric, non-correlating asset, meaning its price movements may not align with those of traditional stocks or bonds.

Investors and institutions are increasingly considering Bitcoin as a means of diversifying their investment portfolios.

$$$ Adoption by the entry of institutional investors, hedge funds, and publicly traded companies into the Bitcoin space suggests a growing acceptance of Bitcoin as a legitimate asset class. This includes investments in Bitcoin as a potential treasury reserve asset. In the derivatives markets, the development of Bitcoin futures and options markets provides tools for hedging and trading, contributing to the establishment of Bitcoin as a financial instrument.

$$$ Bitcoin has gained recognition on a global scale, with regulatory frameworks and acceptance in many various countries. This recognition contributes to its status as a new asset class. Typically, a new asset class would accumulate a flush of new cash—a lot of fresh cash, for conversion.

Criticisms

While widely praised for its innovation and potential, Bitcoin has faced various criticisms over the years.

Bitcoin is known for its price volatility. Critics argue that this volatility can make it challenging for Bitcoin to serve as a stable store of value or a reliable medium of exchange. The rapid price fluctuations can discourage its use in everyday transactions. You should ignore price volatility and become a HODLer to lock in massive gains over time. Within Bitcoin mining, the process by which new Bitcoins are created and transactions are verified requires significant computational power. Critics argue that the energy consumption associated with Bitcoin mining is environmentally unsustainable and contributes to carbon emissions. This has been strongly distorted and conserves power with the strategic use of stranded energy. It further promotes energy production in regions with the most need. To put it in a global perspective, a total of just north of 0.1% of energy is used in Bitcoin mining today. This is far less than what is required to "keep the books right" in traditional banks. The latest United Nations study examining the energy consumption of Bitcoin mining has revealed substantial flaws that question the paper's validity. Major oversights were noted by both the authors and the peer reviewers. The study, which calls for urgent regulatory intervention, doesn't possess the nuanced understanding required for such an intricate issue; this is just to allow woke protestors to produce FUD.

Scalability

It has been said that Bitcoin's blockchain has a limited capacity to process transactions, which is technically accurate, leading to scalability challenges. Without delving too deeply into this issue, layer two or the Lightning Network, can process transactions 10,000 times faster than Visa/MasterCard. While Bitcoin's blockchain has faced scalability challenges, various scaling solutions and layer-two technologies proficiently address this issue and improve transaction throughput; the Lightning Network was tailor-made for Bitcoin. It is not widely understood yet, but Bitcoin was meant to be a store of value, not a currency. The Lightning Network runs Bitcoin now as a currency.

Some critics argue that the relative lack of regulatory oversight in the Bitcoin space can lead to concerns about fraud and market manipulation. This perceived lack of regulation may discourage institutional participation; Bitcoin has a rigid set of self-regulating rules no one can alter except by consensus. Consensus is an active participation to agree on something by the owners and miners.

Bitcoin transactions are irreversible, meaning that once confirmed, they cannot be undone. While this characteristic enhances security, it can be problematic in cases of accidental transactions, as funds cannot be recovered unless you ask nicely.

Bitcoin has, at times, been associated with illicit activities due to its pseudonymous nature. Critics argue that the perceived anonymity can be exploited for money laundering, tax evasion, or other illegal activities, even though, unlike cash, blockchain transactions are transparent and traceable.

Misconceptions

Bitcoin is often associated with illegal activities due to its early use on the Dark-net markets. However, the vast majority of Bitcoin transactions are legitimate. As a matter of fact, dollars are nominally and by percentage far, far more prominent in nefarious transactions. Bitcoin is widely used for investment, remittances, and as a store of value. The perception of Bitcoin as a tool for illegal activities is misconception propaganda.

Critics argue that Bitcoin has no intrinsic value and is purely speculative. While Bitcoin doesn't possess tangible assets like gold, its value is derived from its utility as a decentralized and scarce digital asset, akin to the value assigned to precious metals via open markets. Bitcoin is supported by the largest network in the world both in size and computing power, dwarfing all others. This network is growing exponentially. This is considered value today— value in an unsurpassed network.

Bitcoin Shifts Power Away From Centralized Banks

Yes, one of the fundamental principles and goals of Bitcoin is to shift power away from centralized banks and create a decentralized financial system. Bitcoin is giving all of its power directly back to the owners. This is a done deal regardless of its recognition; through faith and consensus in a working money.

Bitcoin operates on a decentralized network of computers, known as nodes, which collectively validate and record transactions. Tens of thousands of private individuals possess these blockchain nodes, sharing them with the Bitcoin community and constantly comparing them for exactitude and fidelity. This eliminates any need for a central authority, such as a central bank, to control or regulate the currency.

Bitcoin's fixed supply prevents arbitrary increases in the money suppliers.

Bitcoin transactions are designed to be censorship-resistant. Once a transaction is included in a block and added to the blockchain, it becomes a permanent and tamper-resistant record. This feature makes it enigmatical for central authorities to control or censor transactions.

Bitcoin provides financial services to individuals needing access to traditional banking systems. People in regions with limited banking infrastructure or those facing financial exclusion can use Bitcoin as a means of transferring and storing value without relying on banks, which is starting to sound like a dirty word.

Bitcoin users have direct control over their funds through private keys. This contrasts with traditional banking systems, where individuals rely on third-party institutions to manage and secure their money.

Bitcoin operates on a global scale and can be accessed by anyone with an Internet connection. This accessibility reduces the reliance on specific national currencies and the banking system. The fact is that when the bank has your money, they own it. You may have limited access to the money, but they own and control it.

Bitcoin is here, it is now, and it will change everything!

Traditional Financial Systems at Risk

The emergence and adoption of cryptocurrencies, including Bitcoin, have prompted discussions about the potential impact on traditional financial systems.

Some view Bitcoin as a disruptive force that provokes traditional financial systems. Blockchain technology's decentralized nature introduces new financial service models that compete with or complement existing systems. Bitcoin does not require banks or the dollar to leave town by sunset. Only you, the owners of dollars, have that power. I suspect a parallel system will run for a while until it does not—fair warning, though: Bitcoin wears a bulletproof vest.

Others see the rise of Bitcoin as a source of innovation that could lead to improvements in traditional financial systems. Blockchain technology, for example, has the potential to enhance transparency, security, and efficiency in various financial processes.

Central Bank Digital Currencies (CBDCs) might be foisted upon us in a desperate act unless some superior, excellent, better money comes along. Let's pray that Bitcoin is recognized as such before CBDCs gain any traction. The development of Central Bank Digital Currencies (code for spy on us) by central banks is seen by some as a response to the perceived threat from Bitcoin. CBDCs aim to provide the benefits of digital currency within a controlled and regulated framework that offers the same "benefits" as the dollar. Assuming it is not dressed as a red herring already. Doubling down on the integration of CBDCs as a way for traditional financial systems to incorporate digital innovation while maintaining control, while the "perceived threat" is actually to the regulator's livelihood, not the public.

Traditional financial systems face competition from alternative financial systems built on blockchain technology and Bitcoin. Remember that blockchain technology was created by Bitcoin. The manipulators would pry the two apart and offer blockchain as a standalone with their CBDC layer.

Divers opinions suggest the potential for coexistence, where traditional and decentralized financial systems complement each other, perhaps for a short time until the vermin are ferreted out.

Hyperinflation or QE

Traditional financial systems can face challenges related to hyperinflation and quantitative easing (QE), depending on how much QE is injected into our economy. QE is a typical precursor to hyperinflation. Hyperinflation, defined as an extraordinarily high and typically accelerating inflation rate, erodes the value of a country's currency rapidly. In such scenarios, traditional financial systems struggle with price stability, loss of confidence in the currency, and severe disruptions in economic activities. Venezuela has faced one of the most severe cases of hyperinflation in recent history.   Zimbabwe, Argentina, Turkey, and Iran have faced tough economic challenges in recent memory. If you believe the economic debt clock, then the USA also, soon enough. Sooner, if you don't believe it.

QE is a monetary policy tool where central banks purchase financial assets to increase the money supply in an "attempt to stimulate" economic activity.   While QE aims to prevent deflation and support economic growth, it can lead to concerns about asset bubbles, distortions in financial markets, and potential long-term consequences of defunct currency. Excuse me, but does anyone have Everclear to add to the gigantic punchbowl? Stimulus anyone?

In addition to countries with severe inflation or hyperinflation, larger countries are suffering the same fate. For example, the Japanese yen lost 30% of its value last year. The USA is more challenging to see as we export our inflation. The dollar is the cleanest shirt in the hamper, but just look around.   My home purchased about three years ago for 290k is now priced at almost 1 million today. This might be inflation.   We homeowners feel rich but guess what; property tax keeps rising. And I am not rich enough to maintain my home and pay the increasing property taxes, too. I suspect others are in the same boat. I pray that they can swim. But wait, there's more.... The standard way manipulators take from the poor and give to the rich is through credit contraction and expansion cycles, like in the great depression. They control the printing press, and they use it too.

Bitcoin as a Reserve Currency

Bitcoin has gained recognition and consideration primarily as a store of value rather than a traditional currency, even though the second-layer Lightning Network serves as an excellent transactional platform for Bitcoin. Here are some key points regarding Bitcoin's role as a store of value and the potential for it to become a reserve currency. Bitcoin is often referred to as "digital gold" as gold has been a **store of value** for centuries.

Bitcoin's price history, with periods of more than significant appreciation, has attracted long-term investors who believe in its potential as a store of value.

Bitcoin has global recognition enough to *become* a reserve asset; it typically needs international recognition, acceptance, and stability. Bitcoin's global recognition has grown but still lacks widespread acceptance for everyday transactions. This is not required as Bitcoin can be held like gold by the Federal Reserve, which is not used as an everyday vehicle of transaction, even though the Lightning Network makes transactions a breeze. However, I agree that transitioning to a new reserve currency involves overcoming the inertia of existing systems. Unfortunately, regulatory hurdles could influence its trajectory.

Time will tell, But Bitcoin really isn't looking for approval.

Can Quantum Computers Crash Bitcoin?

Quantum computers have an inappreciable potential to impact certain cryptographic algorithms currently used in securing Bitcoin, not in the near term but potentially well down the road. The most notable algorithm at risk is the widely used public-key cryptography algorithm called RSA (Rivest–Shamir–Adleman), which forms the basis for digital signatures and key exchange protocols.

If ever sufficiently advanced, Quantum computers could employ Shor's algorithm to efficiently factor large numbers, breaking the security assumptions underlying RSA. However, Bitcoin uses a higher security, the elliptic curve digital signature algorithm (ECDSA), for its cryptographic signatures, which is currently considered resistant to Shor's algorithm.

While ECDSA is considered quantum-resistant, the cryptographic community acknowledges a negligible potential threat posed by quantum computers to existing encryption standards. As a response, there is ongoing research into quantum-resistant cryptographic algorithms that could withstand attacks from quantum computers. If needed, the development and implementation of these quantum-resistant algorithms would be crucial to maintaining the security of Bitcoin, and other cryptographic systems, in a distant future era of capable quantum computing.

It's important to note that building large-scale, practical quantum computers is a complex engineering challenge. No quantum computer has been developed that poses an immediate threat to Bitcoin or other widely used cryptographic systems. Indeed, the traditional banking system is far more insecure and vulnerable than the elliptic curve digital signature algorithm (ECDSA). The systems pervasive in the world's banks and banking security today would act as a canary in the coal mine for Bitcoin. Again, Bitcoin may be the answer to the "quantum quandary."

FASB

$$$ The Financial Accounting Standards Board (FASB) is a private, non-profit organization in the United States that establishes and improves accounting standards through its Generally Accepted Accounting Principles (GAAP). Fair accounting for Bitcoin involves marking an asset to its current market value (mark-to-market). This is particularly relevant for financial statements and reporting, ensuring that the value reflects the latest market conditions rather than only losses being recognized. Fair accounting, as guided by FASB and GAAP, involves the application of consistent and unbiased principles to ensure that financial statements accurately represent an entity's financial position. Corporations, for the most part, cannot own Bitcoin because of its unfair tax treatment. The truth of FASB will change all that. Corporations far and wide will

come out of the woodwork in search of Bitcoin crumbs to put on their balance sheets. Not just the DOW or NASDAQ, but every small to midsized corporation, too.

Fair accounting can include properly recognizing gains or losses on the asset in financial statements. This would have been a deterrent to corporations from even obtaining or keeping Bitcoin on their balance sheets. Now, things are changing. You will see many, if not most, companies purchase Bitcoin. Companies placing Bitcoin on their balance sheets will cause immense buying pressure. As a matter of fact, it would be unwise for any fiduciary to resist and advise against a Bitcoin position. As they say in the Bitcoin universe, "resistance is futile."

10x Demand Increase and a 50% Decrease at the Halving

$$$ This scenario involves demand for Bitcoin to increase by a factor of 10, which would lead to a substantial increase in price. Increased demand puts substantial upward pressure on prices, assuming the supply remains constant. Currently, Bitcoin purchases of less than one whole Bitcoin amount to Bitcoin purchases of about 700 per day and increasing. This number does not count any institutional purchases. But a simultaneous 50% decrease at the halving, or about 450 per day, will create increased scarcities and unilaterally lead to tremendous upward

price movements. Combining these two scenarios would result in unimaginable price growth on its own. Institutional purchases for everything else, whether it be for pensions, trusts, 401k, ETFs or sovereigns, hedge funds, or the cherry on top of the rest of the world, will magnify the price. I personally have trouble comprehending the possibilities.

Paper Wallet

Using a paper wallet can be considered a method to secure long-term storage of Bitcoin. This is the most simple-to-understand wallet, composed of a key pair. Each key pair consists of a public key and a corresponding private key. The public key is used for encryption and is freely shared, while the private key, which is kept secure and confidential, is utilized for decryption. Example below:

PUBLIC   ADDRESS-

1KTFKJAVBYX9NKDIHU3G6ESCABFGVNEGQ

AND THE CORRESPONDING

PRIVATE-KEY

KYWFMHAE8UR2TZX6EBNTT9VBZVEAZAG3F85JPF7TR5

WCE-CHVVSWEK

This is a working key pair. I recommend that you **do not use it!** Because the private key has been exposed.

Paper wallets are a form of "cold storage," meaning the private keys are generated and stored offline, reducing the risk of exposure to online threats like hacking.

Users have complete control over the generation and storage of the private keys. This provides a level of independence from online wallets or exchanges.

Since the private keys are not connected to the Internet until the paper wallet is used to make a transaction, they are impervious to online hacking attempts. It is highly recommended and super safe *if done correctly*.

The security of a paper wallet largely depends on the precautions taken during its creation. The paper wallet should be generated on a secure, malware-free computer, and the process should be executed in a very secure environment, never touching the Internet during the creation of these *Key Pairs*. This environment should be completely free of any possible intrusion. Intrusions are more prevalent than you can possibly imagine. Do not allow anything to touch the Internet while creating your private keys. I TEND TO REPEAT MYSELF DURING CRUCIAL ISSUES LIKE THIS.

The average person doesn't need to airgap a computer. This is primarily the domain of corporations and governments; it could be a sensitive project or database system for a corporation running an industrial process.

When you airgap a computer, there's nothing between the computer and the rest of the world but air. When WiFi came along, airgapping has been changed to mean no connection to the outside world whatsoever. Nothing that isn't already on the computer should be able to get on it, and nothing on the computer should be able to be taken off of it.

Airgapping a computer is more complex than just unplugging the network cable and disabling the WiFi. Remember, Bitcoin is a high-value target for criminal hackers and Nation-State Actors (NSAs) who work for foreign governments. They've got money and time.

Drones can, and will fly over your home and suck a wallet file from your computer router and later attempt to brute force the password. This cannot be done with a properly prepared paper wallet. BUT NO SHORT CUTS!

Being a physical document, a paper wallet is susceptible to physical damage, loss, or deterioration over time. Protecting it from physical threats is crucial. You could etch your keys into an aluminum strip to protect them from fire or water damage.

A paper wallet for transactions is less convenient than using a digital wallet. In fact, I wouldn't touch my paper wallets until Bitcoin is well north of $500,000.00. Importing private keys from a paper wallet into a software wallet requires careful handling. Creating multiple copies and securely storing them in at least two different locations, (not in the same house) is essential.

I recommend using a paper wallet for many reasons.

1. They are securely offline.

2. They encourage you to be a HODLer as they require an extra step to be spent.

3. As mentioned earlier, Bitcoin is a reserve asset, not a currency. For best performance, pretend your Bitcoin is a five-year CD.

4. Security of your life savings is paramount.

5. Simplicity of a key pair printed on paper.

6. Your keys can be imported to an advanced HD wallet, which will be perfected just in time for your spending spree.

7. Once your paper wallets are created, they can be seamlessly funded without digging up or removing your keys, because the only thing needed to fund your paper wallet is the public address, which corresponds to your safely stored private key.

Users need to have a good understanding of how to obtain, use, and secure a paper wallet. More detailed information will be provided later in this book.

Alternative solutions include hardware wallets (dedicated devices designed for secure Bitcoin storage), a popular and user-friendly alternative to paper wallets. They offer added security features, such as PIN protection and recovery phrases, and are resilient to physical damage. Personally, I don't trust them. Ledger, a hardware wallet, has been outed as a faulty system. For the most part, if you want to sleep well, use desktop and hardware wallets only when you completely understand them and trust them. In the meantime, **Paper Wallets** are easy-peasy and much more secure.

Ultimately, the choice of storage method depends on individual preferences, technical proficiency, and the level of security desired. Whichever method is chosen, it's crucial to stay informed about best practices and regularly review and update security measures. You could easily do it yourself by going to bitaddress.org, creating entropy, and whipping out a key pair. But if it is not air-gapped, you have a chance of a myriad of malware or key-loggers discovering your private key. Remember, air-gapping is simply creating those key pairs without EVER allowing the private key to touch the Internet, and then cold storage it. Key pairs consist of an address and a private key. The address is open to the world because you must provide it for someone to send Bitcoin to you or fund it. The corresponding private key is your key to ownership and the ability/authority to send /transfer the balance of your wallet to another address.

Caution: This transfer should be done only once from your paper wallet, potentially to your own spend hot wallet, but if it is more than you wish to keep in a hot or warm wallet, then you should send it back to another paper wallet key pair. It is really quite simple but highly critical to get it right.

Permutations of Private Keys

There are 10 million million million million million million million million, or 115,792,089,237,316,195,423,570,985,008,687,907,852,-837,564,279,074,904,382,605,163,141,518,161,494,225 possible private keys. The number of possible keys is so large that the security of Bitcoin relies on the assumption that no one will ever, ever, ever generate the same two private keys twice. This number is more than all of the atoms in the visible universe.

I am not going to discuss the exact mechanisms of the design or the protocol of Bitcoin here, but I thought it was worth feeling a piece of the blueprint. Let's face it: none of us understand how email works, yet we use it every day.

Absolutely Secure and Simple

At the end of this book, I will recommend a simple way to secure a paper wallet key pair that has been air-gapped and kept anonymous. I recommend getting Bitcoin and holding it ASAP, even a tiny amount. Next, learn about Bitcoin. Usually, I would recommend learning first, but you will learn faster if you purchase $10 or $50 of Bitcoin and store it, then learn faster.

Full Control and Direct Ownership: Owning Bitcoin in self-custody means having complete control over the asset with no counterparty risk and no yearly fees ever again. All of the freedoms ride on the back of direct ownership and control of Bitcoin.

Metrics in Bitcoin

 Bitcoin has various metrics which provide insights into its network, market, and overall health. Here are some of the primary metrics you can use to analyze and assess Bitcoin:

Price Metrics: The current market price of one Bitcoin.

Market Capitalization: The total value of all Bitcoins in circulation, calculated by multiplying the current price by the total supply.

Network Metrics: The pace of growth of the Bitcoin network.

Hash Rate: The total computational power dedicated to mining and securing the Bitcoin network.

Difficulty: A measure of how hard it is to find a new block, adjusted approximately every two weeks based on the network's hash rate.

Block Height: The number of blocks in the blockchain, indicating the length of the chain.

Supply Metrics

Circulating Supply: The total number of Bitcoins in circulation at a given time.

Transaction Metrics

Transactions Per Day/Second: The number of Bitcoin transactions occurring over a specific period.

Transaction Fees: The fees users pay for transactions to be included in a block.

Security Metrics:

Security audits and vulnerability assessments conducted by independent firms help identify and mitigate potential weaknesses in software implementations and infrastructure services, thereby improving overall network security.

Block Confirmations: The number of subsequent blocks added to the block containing a particular transaction, providing increased security over time.

Mining Reward: The reward given to miners for successfully adding a new block to the blockchain. This reward includes newly created Bitcoins and transaction fees.

Market Metrics

Trading Volume: The total value of Bitcoin traded in a specific period.

Dominance: Bitcoin's market dominance percentage indicates its share of the total cryptocurrency market capitalization.

Sentiment Metrics: for discussions, sentiments, and trends related to Bitcoin.

Social Media Activity: Monitoring social media platforms.

Google Trends: Analyzing the popularity of searches for "Bitcoin" on Google, reflecting public interest.

Adoption Metrics

Wallets: The number of active Bitcoin wallets and wallet providers.

Merchant Adoption: The number of businesses accepting Bitcoin for goods and services.

These metrics provide a comprehensive view of Bitcoin from various angles, including its economic, technical, and social aspects. Analyzing these metrics can help investors and analysts better understand the current state and trends of the Bitcoin ecosystem.

Asset Classes

Asset classes are broad categories of financial instruments that share similar behaviors and characteristics in the financial markets. The main asset classes include:

Equities (Stocks):

Ownership shares in a company represent a claim on part of the company's assets and earnings. If you are really good, stocks may keep up with inflation, but let's face it: a stockholder waits on the FED to loosen monetary policy more while he sits on a cliff of impending doom. I am reminded of the story of Sisyphus, a character from Greek mythology. Sisyphus was a king whose punishment for his deceitful behavior was condemned by the gods to roll a boulder up a hill endlessly. However, each time he neared the top, the boulder would roll back down, and Sisyphus would have to repeat the task for eternity.

<u>Fixed-Income Securities (Bonds):</u>

Bonds cannot keep up with inflation. Debt instruments where investors lend money to an issuer government, corporation, or other entities in exchange for periodic interest payments and the return of principal at maturity. These, too, are precariously perched. These are subject to inflation, bankruptcy and things such as war; low risk, but even lower return.

<u>Real Estate:</u>

Including physical properties, residential, commercial, and industrial real estate, and others. Potential for rental income, capital appreciation, and diversification. Risks include real estate taxes, vandalism, maintenance, law, eminent domain, zoning rule changes, and tenant headaches. Not to mention Covid.

<u>Commodities</u>: include physical goods, gold, silver, oil, agricultural products, etc. These all take work and are subject to price swings and price manipulation. They can act as a hedge against inflation.

<u>Hedge Funds</u>: are pooled investment funds that employ various strategies to generate returns.

<u>Derivatives:</u> Financial contracts whose value is derived from an underlying asset. Includes options, futures, swaps, and added risk.

<u>Collectibles and Art Investments:</u> These are definitely not liquid and, in tough economic times, can lose most of their

value. Items of value such as art, rare stamps, vintage cars, and other collectibles. These hold a limited and subjective matter.

<u>And now comes Bitcoin:</u> Bitcoin requires 10 to 100 hours of education. But all of the negative attachments above have disappeared. The earlier you purchase Bitcoin, the more appreciation you will receive on a four-year time horizon which correlates with the natural halving cycle. No one who properly secured their Bitcoin has ever lost money through theft or inflation; there are no headaches, and volatility and price manipulation are self-correcting. This asset has a decentralized nature; it also possesses a potential for extreme capital appreciation, assuming you have properly secured your Bitcoin.

These asset classes serve different investment objectives and risk tolerances. Diversification across multiple asset classes is a common strategy to manage risk and enhance portfolio stability. Investors often allocate their portfolios based on their financial goals, time horizon, and risk appetite. But I would rethink my understanding or attraction to these asset classes in light of the new kid on the blockchain. When secured properly, Bitcoin has no risk of confiscation, less risk of being taxed, no inflation, no management risk, no work to maintain, no counterparty risk, and a high potential of increasing in value substantially over the coming years and decades. Historically, Bitcoin has appreciated far more than any other asset given any 4-year time horizon, with an average of over 200% year over year.

The First Published Exchange Rate

The first known published exchange rate of Bitcoin (BITCOIN) to U.S. dollars occurred on October 5, 2009. At that time, the first recorded Bitcoin exchange rate was established on the now-famous BitcoinMarket.com, a platform created by software developer Jed McCaleb. The initial price was set at 1,309.03 BTC (bitcoins) for 1 USD (U.S. dollar).

To calculate the percentage appreciation, you can use the formula:

Percentage Appreciation=(Final Value−Initial ValueInitial Value)×100Percentage Appreciation=(Initial ValueFinal Value−Initial Value)×100

In this case:

· Initial Value (IV) is 0.00076413 or 1309 Btc for a dollar

· Final Value (FV) is $44,000. Per Btc (at the time of this writing)

Now, let's plug these values into the formula:

Percentage

Appreciation=(44,000−0.00076413)×100Percentage Appreciation= (0.0007641344,000−0.00076413)×100

Percentage

Appreciation=(43,999.999235870.00076413)×100Percent age Appreciation=(0.0007641343,999.99923587)×100 Percentage Appreciation≈5,756,079,625%

So, the percentage appreciation, starting from an initial value of 0.00076413 or 1309 BTC for a dollar and ending at $44,000 per Btc, is (5,756,079,625%).

It's better than my dad's series EE bonds, which is approximately a 14-year track record. Sure, past performance is not an indicator of future results, but come on!! Bitcoin is now being considered an asset class, adopted by the institutions and clamored for by them in a dog-eat-dog competition. They are trying to keep you out with bogus regulation news, FUD, and nervous propaganda,

Past performance is not a guarantee of future results. This mantra and standard disclaimer in the investment industry is meant to convey that just because an asset, such as Bitcoin or any other investment, has performed in a stellar way in the past, it doesn't guarantee that it will continue to do so in the future. I contend that there has never been a more critical time considering how early and young this asset class is and what it will do to all other asset classes— especially all forms of almost worthless fiat. Trust is waning for them just to survive. Bitcoin is trustless and permissionless.

Glassnode Analytics

Glassnode is a blockchain analytics and intelligence platform. Reports of heightened inflows from institutional sources into Bitcoin, which suggests continued interest and participation from institutional and retail investors into Bitcoin, are piling up. Institutional involvement in the Bitcoin space has been a notable trend in very recent years, with institutional investors, hedge funds, and corporations showing increased interest in Bitcoin as a store of value and to extinguish inflation. Factors, such as the growing acceptance of Bitcoin by mainstream financial institutions, the development of cryptocurrency-related financial products, and "regulatory clarity" in some jurisdictions, have contributed to this trend. This trend explicitly denotes the more significant movement and provides a pile-on effect for Bitcoin's price advancement.

Please note that when I write, I have to tell you two things: the mass perception, and what is true. Usually, I will quote a word or a phrase, as my eyes roll back in my head, when it is mass perception.

Gold Exchange-Traded Fund (ETF)

$$$ A historical look back at the price of gold. The first gold exchange-traded fund (ETF) was launched in 2003.

The SPDR Gold Shares (GLD) was the pioneer in this space and became the first physically backed gold ETF. State Street Global Advisors introduced it and began trading on the New York Stock Exchange (NYSE) on November 18, 2004. The historical performance of other assets, like gold, after the introduction of an ETF (Exchange-Traded Fund) does not guarantee similar outcomes for Bitcoin. However, we can analyze the factors influencing Bitcoin's price in the context of a probable ETF debut. Gold's ETF began in 2004: GLD was launched in November 2004, so this year has no full-year return.

2005: 18.31%

2006: 23.97%

2007: 31.44%

2008: 5.84%

2009: 24.33%

2010: 29.27%

2011: 9.57%

The introduction of gold ETFs, particularly the SPDR Gold Shares, provided investors with a new way to gain exposure to the price of gold without physically owning and storing the precious metal. These ETFs are designed to track the price of gold and are "ostensibly" backed by physical gold held in vaults. It is not a conspiracy theory if it is true!

Since the launch of the first gold ETF, several other similar products have been introduced in various markets, offering investors additional options to include gold in their portfolios. Gold ETFs have gained popularity as a convenient and liquid way for both retail and institutional investors to invest in gold, without dealing with the logistics of owning and storing physical gold. We are the government, and we are here to help. I remain dubious. The gold price rose 400% after the gold ETF in 2004. What do you think Bitcoin will do in 2024 after its ETF debut occurs? I want to caution all ETF investors of counterparty risk, and many, like me, do not believe that gold exists in proportion to the gold ETF. Gold has been rehypothecated so many times that there is no actual way to keep track. The SEC does nothing while 100 to 500 times paper gold remains unbacked and unaudited. This is far more difficult to happen to Bitcoin, but **will** happen eventually to the Bitcoin spot ETF despite the rules. Remember, governments have a nose for assets collected in one area or "Honeypot." Ask your asset management firm about Bitcoin if the custodian who held keys, ostensibly for you, is protected from government confiscation. Are they 100% seizure proof? Ask about 6102. I do not think so! My advice is to buy Bitcoin and self-custody.

Executive Order 6102, signed by President Franklin D. Roosevelt on April 5, 1933, was an order that prohibited the hoarding of gold coins, gold bullion, and gold certificates within the United States. The order required individuals, partnerships, associations, and corporations to deliver all gold coins, gold bullion, and gold certificates owned by them, to the Federal Reserve by May 1, 1933. This executive order was issued as part of Roosevelt's efforts to address the banking crisis and stabilize the economy during the Great Depression. Some say this was not a confiscation. I would differ with them. All were offered $20 per oz. and shortly after that, gold rose to $35 per oz; a full 40% confiscation.

An ETF would make it easier for institutional and retail investors to gain exposure to an already exploding asset; with the ETF owning the index of Bitcoin, without directly owning and managing the asset would massively increase demand. This, in turn, will shoot the Bitcoin price up, and if you follow my thesis, given some time, it will **never** come down again. In my opinion, this beautiful honeypot of low-hanging fruit will be replaced with fractionalized treasuries. Your only protection will be to educate yourself and self-custody.

Positive sentiment surrounding the approval and launch of a Bitcoin ETF could attract more and more investors to the market. The word on the street is several billions of dollars injected on day one. Given two years, it will be an order of magnitude higher. Although I am concerned with a GBTC dump initially. The Grayscale Bitcoin Trust, is a publicly traded company that allows investors to gain exposure to the price movements of Bitcoin, without having to buy it directly themselves. Grayscale Investments, the company behind GBTC, manages the trust. Although investors believe in Bitcoin, they have paid enormous daily fees, hence the likely exodus. That will work itself out in short order, though. Most, if not all, those dollars will be reinjected into the ETF, essentially with a tenth of GBTC's fees, with no restrictions. The Bitcoin ETF will then rise in a massive crescendo of gains over the next three or four years and beyond. I would not wait and see because some entity is going to get in on those GBTC Bitcoin outflows.

To calculate the market capitalization of physical gold at a price of $2,100 per ounce, you would use the formula:

Market Cap=Gold Price per Ounce × Total Ounces in Existence Market Cap=Gold Price per Ounce × Total Ounces in Existence

As mentioned before, determining the total ounces of gold in existence can vary based on different estimates. A commonly cited figure is around 200,000 metric tons. Let's use that as a rough estimate:

{Market Cap} = $2,100/oz \times 200,000 \ { metric tons} \times 32,150 \

 { ounces/metric ton}

Then divide 13 trillion by 21,000,000 Bitcoin, and each would be worth $640,000.00. As much as I love gold, Bitcoin has much more utility and security. Gold has been plundered and sacked over and over throughout history. Even though you hear about Bitcoin exchanges faltering, it has no bearing on the Bitcoin system, which has never been hacked or looted. It is people's perception that things associated with Bitcoin *are* Bitcoin. This is absolutely not true, and the manipulators love to perpetuate such things; so they can enrich themselves. If you truly understood the distributed ledger, you can see that everyone could own Bitcoin, which is not true of gold.

MicroStrategy as a Good Proxy for Bitcoin

MicroStrategy (MSTR) is a business intelligence and software company that has gained attention in the digital currency space for its significant investment in Bitcoin. MicroStrategy's CEO, Michael Saylor, has been vocal about his bullish stance on Bitcoin, and the company has made significant investments in the digital currency as part of its treasury strategy.

MicroStrategy's stock performance is influenced by its unique structure, which allows it to buy Bitcoin. Its core business operations include the market dynamics of the business intelligence sector. The company has become a notable proxy for Bitcoin due to its substantial holdings. Movements can influence the value of MicroStrategy's stock in the price of Bitcoin, and investors who are interested in gaining exposure to Bitcoin indirectly may consider MicroStrategy as one of the very few publicly traded companies with a significant Bitcoin position, currently about 1% of all Bitcoin. Most recently, Michael

Saylor has said he intends to acquire 5% of Bitcoins, a whole 21,000,000 Bitcoins, which amounts to more than one million Bitcoins. I consider this superior to the Bitcoin ETF, depending on shares to Bitcoin ratio. But this still acts as an index of the underlying asset. To calculate the ratio, divide the value of MicroStrategy's Bitcoin holdings by the current market price of one share. This will give you an approximate ratio of Bitcoin holdings to MicroStrategy shares. I hope you are starting to understand that the demand is higher than there are Bitcoins to go around. In fact, if or when everyone in the world were to buy some Bitcoin, there would only be enough to provide about two-thousandths of a Bitcoin each: 0.002625 BTC or about $100 worth today. Unfortunately, most Bitcoins have been bought up and HODLed.

The ETF Will Produce Inflows of Billions into Bitcoin Daily

$$$ The impact of a $1,000,000,000.00 inflow into Bitcoin without any outflows, would depend on several factors, and predicting the exact outcome is provocative due to the market's fledgling understanding of the Bitcoin market. However, we can consider general aspects. This exercise is simply to try and gauge the potential price action.

A $1 billion inflow is a significant amount. Still, numbers much larger and multiples of the same will be competing for unavailable Bitcoin in a reduced availability market, where the asset's ask cannot be found, especially in size. It will lead to an unequivocal violent upside on the price. The larger the market capitalization of Bitcoin, the higher the competition will escalate. In my mind's eye, I foresee a membership required to even bid on this asset in the near future. All this will contribute to $$$.

Sideliners Remorse

Eventually, the liquidity of the market will stack, searching for any available seller; and provide sideliners remorse, with weeping and gnashing of teeth because of their indecision. Bitcoin price chasing will ensue. Notice that I said chasing, not catching an ask.

A perfect storm is coming; perceived worthless cash and a reduced natural supply of Bitcoin due to the coming halving, positive news or a bullish market sentiment could attract more and more buyers. Adding to the list is FOMO on steroids, potentially contributing to stratospheric price movement. Add BlackRock's ETF producing only inflows, and 14 other asset management fund managers' unidirectional AUM, rolling in faster and higher than the gold market itself; being a 14 trillion dollar market. Add to that the incoming central banks and sovereign countries' "eureka moment." Do you get my drift? Certain institutions are desperate for Bitcoin in size. This is coming, too; others will wake up as FOMO begets FOMO.

The psychological impact of such a substantial inflow might also have a FOMO impact on the balance of the market, influencing their perception of Bitcoin's value and potential future price movements.

Much MO FOMO. Look, this is a done deal, except for the cheering and shouting.

This is just a pre-summary of how Bitcoin's violent upside will unfold.

Will Normalcy Bias Evaporate?

For today's traditional financial markets, normalcy bias will eventually evaporate in favor of Bitcoin.

Predicting the timing for a shift in sentiment from traditional financial markets to Bitcoin is inherently perplexing. The adoption and acceptance of Bitcoin as a viable asset class and store of value are subjectively done. But the "normalcy bias," which refers to the tendency of individuals to underestimate the possibility of disruptive events, will linger. Normalcy bias tends to cling to the belief that existing conditions will persist forever. What a dramatic dichotomy in the context of traditional financial markets and Bitcoin; a shift away from traditional economic norms in favor of Bitcoin could occur somewhere right between gradually and suddenly.

Schizophrenic

Will the schizophrenic love/hate relationship with the dollar lead to speedier adoption of Bitcoin? This one is for you to decide.

The relationship between the United States and its national currency, the U.S. Dollar (USD), is indeed complex and can be characterized by a mix of sentiments. The U.S. Dollar is a globally dominant reserve currency; while widely used in international trade, finance, and as a global store of value. Concerns about economic policies and the potential impact of massive monetary stimulus measures have led to debates about the dollar's long-term stability. A wide range of dollar participators, companies, banks, etc., are vested deeply in dollars, even though most countries prefer the dollar over their own currency. The USA, like a rabid dog with a meaty bone mindset is to defend the dollar at all cost; at least in the minds of the master/slave relationship, with the dollar as the master that leaves you, well, you know, dependent on the dollar.

Bitcoin advocates often argue that the decentralized nature and limited supply of Bitcoin fixes money. In a deep-seated way, they are right. This makes it an attractive alternative or supplement to traditional fiat currencies, especially in the context of perceived issues with government-controlled currencies, which are floundering. The dollar is on tilt; it is a melting iceberg in the warm

Caribbean Sea. Very few are aware of it. Make your plans now for either a life raft or a Yacht.

Buying the Rumor and Selling the News

The strategy of "buying the rumor and selling the news" is a shared trading approach, especially in financial markets where significant events or announcements can influence asset prices in the context of a Bitcoin spot ETF approval. This short-term trading tactic might work, but you may get quickly priced out of the market and be in the un-admirable position of chasing the market if you can even catch it. Remember a five billion percent increase since Bitcoins' inception. How will you feel if Bitcoin teleports to $100,000 or $200,000 per Bitcoin, sounds incredible; do the math! Take a look at a chart!

When Bitcoin Matches Golds Market Cap

To calculate the market capitalization of physical gold at a price of $2,100 per ounce, you would use the formula:

Market Cap=Gold Price per Ounce × Total Ounces in Existence Market Cap=Gold Price per Ounce × Total Ounces in Existence

As mentioned before, determining the total ounces of gold

in existence can vary based on different estimates. A commonly cited figure is around 200,000 metric tons. Let's use that as a rough estimate:

{Market Cap} = \$2,100/oz \times 200,000 \ { metric tons} \times 32,150 \

 { ounces/metric ton}

Then divide 13 trillion by 21,000,000 Bitcoin and each would be worth \$640,000.00 As much as I love gold; Bitcoin has much more utility and security. Gold has been plundered and sacked over and over throughout history. Even though you hear about Bitcoin exchanges faltering, it has no bearing on the Bitcoin system which has never been hacked or looted. It is people's perception that things associated with Bitcoin are Bitcoin. This is absolutely not true and the manipulators love to perpetuate such things. So they can enrich themselves. If you truly understood the distributed ledger you could see that everyone could own Bitcoin which is not true of Gold.

Bitcoin's Spot ETF

An exchange-traded fund, or ETF, is a security that tracks a basket of underlying assets or commodities, securities, or a mix of both. ETFs trade on securities exchanges like regular stocks. Ordinary mom-and-pop investors can buy them.

Coiners have long dreamed of Bitcoin having a spot ETF. There's a thought that the moment there's a Bitcoin ETF, the big institutional bucks will flood in! This perception has some truth. But it is a double-edged sword; wrapping the underlying asset, Bitcoin, and selling only the indexed product that tracks Bitcoin in dollars, which forfeits most of the other attributes of Bitcoin. Bitcoin is a custodian-held asset in the ETF, and never the twain, you and the Bitcoin, shall meet. You will miss out on the other attributes.

The first proposal for a Bitcoin spot ETF was submitted by the investment firm VanEck in 2017—the proposed ETF, known as the VanEck SolidX.

Then, Cameron and Tyler Winklevoss submitted a proposal for a Bitcoin spot ETF. The SEC nixed them also.

Fast forward to August 22, 2018, the SEC rejected nine Bitcoin ETF applications in one day. They claimed they were concerned about the "potential for fraud in the marketplace." This is where I suspect the SEC and manipulators woke up to Bitcoin.

But then, in October 2021, the SEC approved a Bitcoin futures ETF. This, based on the courts judgment that the Chicago Mercantile Exchange Bitcoin futures (unattached Bitcoins) was already running well. The court sent the SEC packing. The Bitcoin prices that CME was using were just as manipulated as any. We suspect the SEC couldn't really refuse the spot ETF because the CME was already highly regulated, and its Bitcoin futures product was fine with the CFTC. So why would a safer, Bitcoin-backed product pose a greater risk for the market? Answer: It didn't, and the court said so. But the court wasn't thinking or talking about the threat it posed to the manipulator's control of money. Someone made a serious political miscalculation.

GBTC

Grayscale's GBTC, which debuted in September 2013, was the closest thing to a spot Bitcoin ETF for many years — only it wasn't one. Unlike an ETF, GBTC is a closed-end fund. Once Bitcoins entered the trust, there was no way to get them out. There was even a rule that the initial buyer of GBTC had to hold GBTC for a specified time.

Grayscale ceased GBTC issuance in March 2021; they could have reversed course to redemption mode. They did not. GBTC maintained a high 2% management fee. Today, GBTC has set fees just prior to the potential spot EFT conversion, at most likely 1.5%. They must believe their GBTC holders are too lazy to switch to a more competitive, 25 basis points or less. Talk about big kahunas.

Because GBTC is a Hotel California for Bitcoins, "you can check out any time you like, but you can never leave;" GBTC has never tried to trade in line with the price of Bitcoin. GBTC traded higher than Bitcoin in 2020 because of subterfuge, but current holders are underwater. There are a lot of angry GBTC holders.

Grayscale applied to convert GBTC into a spot ETF in October 2021, hoping to bring the price of GBTC back up. The SEC rejected their application. Grayscale appealed, saying that the CME Bitcoin futures ETF was allowed if their fraud prevention arrangements passed muster. The same should hold true for Grayscale's proposal. The appeals court agreed that the SEC had unfairly blocked the Grayscale spot Bitcoin ETF. The panel called the order "arbitrary and capricious" because the SEC never explained why it approved indistinguishable products. The SEC would further review Grayscale's bid for a spot ETF. The SEC decided not to appeal, and Grayscale issued a fresh filing in the form of an S-3, with this year's modification as cash only. What a confluence of perfect storms colliding.

Government Monopoly on the Issuance of Money

The quote, "We will not have good money until we get it out of the hands of government," is attributed to Friedrich Hayek, the Austrian-British economist. This sentiment is captured in his writings, particularly in his book "*The Denationalization of Money*." This is now a reality and possible with Bitcoin.

In this work, Hayek argued for the idea that the government monopoly on the issuance of money could be detrimental to the stability and value of currencies. He proposed the concept of competition among private issuers of currencies, saying that this competition would lead to more stable and sound money.

Hayek embraced the reduction of government control over the monetary system.

Amen.

Rehypothecation

Gold can be rehypothecated, but can Bitcoin?

The concept of rehypothecation refers to the practice of using the same collateral for multiple transactions or loans. In traditional financial markets, certain assets, including gold and other commodities, can be subject to rehypothecation under certain conditions. However, Bitcoin operates in a unique digital and decentralized environment, and its characteristics severely limit the extent to which rehypothecation can occur. Rehypothecation cannot be done on layer one of Bitcoin.

Key Points

In the Bitcoin network, ownership is determined by control of private keys. If an individual holds the private keys to a Bitcoin wallet, they have ownership and control over the associated Bitcoins.

Bitcoin operates on a decentralized blockchain, and transactions are recorded on a public ledger. The ownership and transfer of Bitcoins are managed by the network's distributed consensus mechanism, reducing or eliminating the need for intermediaries.

In a business with network effects, the share of organic users relative to paid users (*the ones you spend to acquire*) should increase over time. This is because as the network grows and becomes more valuable for users to join, more organic users should want to participate of their own accord. Bitcoins network is free of charge even as large as this network has grown. Free, when you are not actively using it or just storing it. When you make a transaction, you pay a slight charge to the miner network. Dollars, an extensive network, charge you every day whether you use it or not. So, Bitcoin users are all organic. The network is growing so fast, and the benefit of the network is so vast that it absolutely amazes me that it hasn't already crushed traditional finance. What a wonderful place to be investing.

Some individuals and institutions use custodial services to store and manage their Bitcoins. In such cases, custody providers may hold Bitcoins on behalf of clients. This is where it might get squirrelly. The terms of these custodial arrangements vary, and some may involve lending or rehypothecation of assets. Maybe the custodian drinks; or they can be coerced or blackmailed; my advice is to hold to the maxim "not your keys, not your Bitcoin."

Some platforms offer lending services where users can lend their Bitcoins to other users in exchange for interest. In these cases, the borrowed Bitcoins may be out of your control. Again, "not your keys, not your Bitcoin." Just say no or dive into the details of where the devil resides.

When Bitcoins are held with third-party custodians or lending platforms used for purposes such as trading or short selling, there is a degree of counterparty risk. Users should carefully consider the terms and conditions of such a pact and assess the associated risks. Remember "not your keys, not your Bitcoin."

There is a predetermined, small amount of built-in inflation in Bitcoin to counteract lost coins. This predetermined inflation is fixed, transparent, and finite. This small amount of inflation comes from rewarding the miners and has an end date, meaning fees will take over the job. Bitcoin mining is ever-growing in competition for smaller and smaller rewards. It would then necessarily imply that it is a given that Bitcoin will grow in price ever so much higher.

Bitcoin has a fixed and predictable supply schedule outlined in its code. The rate at which new Bitcoins are created through the mining process is baked into the cake. Bitcoin undergoes a "halving" approximately every four years. This event reduces the reward that miners receive for adding new blocks to the blockchain by half. The purpose of these halvings is to gradually reduce the rate at which new Bitcoins are introduced into circulation, ultimately leading to a maximum supply of 21 million Bitcoins.

The next halving is expected to occur around April, 2024. The exact timing can vary slightly due to the nature of Bitcoin's consensus algorithm and the time it takes to mine a certain number of blocks.

The final Bitcoins are expected to be mined around the year 2140, and the competition stands to be fierce, with only a few Satoshis as a reward. This means each Satoshi is worth 0.00000001 BTC. In order for one Satoshi to be worth one cent, 1 BTC would need to be worth $1 million. I am sure miners will not work for a few cents. Again, do the math. The mining capacity is growing exponentially every day. What do they know?

The average loss rate of Bitcoin can be influenced by factors such as lost private keys, unrecoverable hardware wallets, and other forms of unintentional loss. While it's difficult to quantify the loss rate precisely, it's generally considered that many Bitcoins will be permanently lost over time. However, the impact of these losses on the overall supply is expected to decrease as the total supply approaches 21 million. Side note: Every April 15th, I burn a ceremonious $1 bill to privately rejoice in my understanding of an inflationary system. Does the system give every owner of dollars a piece back? NO! They git my worth-less dolla!

 If I lose a Bitcoin private key or die intestate, every other HODLer gets a share of my Bitcoin. My enslavers get nothing.

In summary, the fully transparent, predetermined inflation of Bitcoin will continue to decrease with each halving event, and it will approach zero by 2140.

I envision a day when there will be a new order book for Bitcoin; one that might be named a "*market plus premium order*" that places you in line for an order before others, by adding a 20% surcharge to your market order. This may allow you into a queue, to patiently wait for some willing sellers.

Even today, the market's willing sellers are thin. It is my contention that a consortium of institutions have colluded to push the price of Bitcoin down by strategically dumping it on the market to demoralize it. This will prompt the market to look away so that a god-candle will happen (transporting Bitcoin to a much higher level). This is not unprecedented and has been something of a common event for coveted issues.

So you ask, where do all these Bitcoins come from allowing these manipulators to bully the table? A little-known fact: Fidelity has been mining Bitcoin almost since its inception. The manipulators, such as BlackRock's CEO Larry Fink, have been deriding Bitcoin for years, while mining it in the back room.

It is now well known that BlackRock has purchased almost half of all publicly owned mining companies. This represents a hefty amount of Bitcoin mining power. What hypocrisy! I guess it is right in his name.

To what end, you ask? The institutions were, for the most part, late to the game and needed to establish their footing. Money is not much of an issue for them; BlackRock alone controls well over 11 trillion dollars of AUM assets under management. This is more dough than many first-world nations.

I have no direct facts on this matter, but obvious patterns emerge when contemplated, fit the mold, and eventually reveal themselves.

The manipulators and even a more spiritually overriding power, seems to be attempting to get weak people to buy the ETF, rather than allow them to control their own private keys.

This will cost the investor a commission, a yearly custodian holding fee, and the risk of regulatory impositions and/or direct theft and/or taxation.

If you must, go ahead and purchase a Bitcoin spot ETF; then, quickly learn about the reasons to control your own keys. It is really not that hard. Then do nothing; sit back, and feel the thrust and trust.

The evolution of Bitcoin will move predominantly towards banks as we know them today, converting to a Bitcoin custodian services; first as an ancillary service to their core service, then a full time job.

The quote "We get the Bitcoin price we deserve" is often attributed to a well-known figure in the cryptocurrency space, Andreas M. Antonopoulos. Andreas Antonopoulos is a prominent Bitcoin advocate, author, and speaker, who has been active in the cryptocurrency community for many years. He is known for his educational efforts to help people understand the principles of Bitcoin and blockchain technology. Andreas Antonopoulos is a great Bitcoin proponent possessing tremendous knowledge in all subject areas. He can be found on YouTube. He can answer many of your varied questions.

FUD stands for "fear, uncertainty, and doubt." FUD will saturate the news, allowing manipulators to sway Bitcoin up and down in volatile swings to their benefit. This communication tactic influences people towards having a contorted perception of something through deliberate misinformation.   This results in a "we told you so" hypocrisy, as they rake in easy profits from the uninformed seekers of easy gain. Owning Bitcoin may be easy, but you can play with your emotions, especially if the convenience and trust in a Bitcoin ETF is the extent of your research. I suggest studying the Bitcoin proposition.

Suppose you are determined to make an ETF purchase and commit to doing it only very temporarily. Then, do the work and educate yourself to self-custody. Then, wait for the rest of the world to finish adopting.

In other words, buy the asset, secure it, and wait for a million dollars per Bitcoin print; then, you should sell a bit for your dreams to be manifested. But, I suggest you do not sell it all! Better yet, use DeFi to borrow against your position, let's say at 4% or 5% interest, to be able to buy nice things. On average, Bitcoin has historically risen more than 200% annually, quickly covering your 5% bank interest, year after year, with a write-off.   Why let the hardest money in the world leave your grasp?

Anywherevillage, Africa

I would think that if Bitcoin FUD propaganda weren't so intense, everyone would wake up to this fairly obvious utopian blessing or at least take the time to appreciate it. Half of what I read online is purposeful misinformation. The human condition lulls the well-off to accept the status quo and tends to ignore all else. Conversely, this provides somewhat of an advantage to third-world citizens. The unbanked have a deep-seated need for Bitcoin. In this relatively advantageous condition, issues of life such as food, clean water, and medical issues will initially hinder the unbanked from utilizing this extreme new advantage. For them, if a way is possible, they will find it. For example, a young man in Anywherevillage, Africa, can purchase a smartphone and act as a bank node to transact all villagers' Bitcoin. With the right wallet, each villager could have their own password to access their keys for signatures of transactions. For the first time in their lives, they will be banked. This advancement will allow most of the world's indigent to save money and own property of their own. Productivity will abound. You might be surprised to see what industrious individuals are capable of, if given the ability to have hard money options.

The Bitcoin Proposition is Enormous

PGP stands for "Pretty Good Privacy," a data encryption/decryption program used for securing emails, files, and other digital communications. PGP was originally developed by Phil Zimmermann in 1991, and it has become a widely used method for protecting sensitive information in the realm of digital privacy and security.

Bitcoin itself does not use PGP (Pretty Good Privacy) directly in its protocol. However, PGP and concepts similar to it can be used in the broader context of securing communications related to Bitcoin transactions and wallet management.

Here's how PGP or similar concepts are relevant in the Bitcoin ecosystem. Secure communication in the Bitcoin ecosystem may use PGP to secure their communications, especially in the context of discussing transactions, wallet management, and other sensitive matters. PGP can be employed to encrypt emails, messages, or other forms of communication.

Bitcoin transactions use a cryptographic concept similar to digital signatures. Each transaction is signed with the private key associated with the sender's Bitcoin address. This process ensures the authenticity and integrity of the transaction. While not PGP, it shares the idea of using cryptographic signatures for verification.

In the realm of securing Bitcoin wallets, PGP or similar technologies may be used to encrypt and secure private keys or mnemonic phrases. This adds an extra layer of protection in case the wallet's data is compromised.

Bitcoin itself relies on its own cryptographic principles, including elliptic curve cryptography for key generation and digital signatures. Bitcoin's security model is based on the decentralized and transparent nature of its blockchain, and the use of cryptographic concepts ensures the integrity of transactions and the ownership of Bitcoins.

Notify Your Heirs

Notifying your heirs about your Bitcoin holdings and ensuring a smooth transition of your digital assets to them involves some planning. While there isn't a specific protocol built into the Bitcoin network for inheritance, there are several practices and tools you can use to achieve this. New features are being updated every day. Time locks and on-chain transfers within the Bitcoin protocol are being improved. And before you are ready to kick the bucket, you should be able to implement them. In the meantime, consult with legal and financial professionals to include your Bitcoin holdings in your estate planning. Bitcoin should be handled after your passing. A simple and quiet passing of the private keys should easily avoid probate and mess. Store important information about your Bitcoin holdings in a secure location or two. This could include details about wallets, private keys, and recovery phrases. Ensure that your heirs know where to find this information when the time comes.

Consider using specialized services that provide tools for digital asset inheritance. These services often use multi-signature wallets or time-locked transactions to facilitate the transfer of assets to designated heirs. Examples include platforms like Casa Covenant and Unchained Capital.

Safe and Secure Under Duress

Use multi-signature wallets (multi-sig) where multiple private keys are required to authorize a transaction. This way, you can enlist trusted individuals or family members as co-signers, ensuring that access to funds requires their participation.

Large firms use multi-signature storage to secure their cold storage Bitcoin. Exchanges, brokers, and the like, distribute admin keys for their funds in order to distribute the risk; if hackers, or worse, want access to their reserves, they're going to need several keys to do so. Similarly, multi-sig ensures no single person in the firm can unilaterally sign transactions from the account. The more signatures you need to execute a transaction, the more the decision-making process can be distributed.

Communicate essential details like this with your heirs. Use encrypted methods such as PGP (Pretty Good Privacy) or secure messaging apps to share sensitive information. Educate yourself, then educate your heirs.

It's crucial to balance security and accessibility when planning for the inheritance of Bitcoin. Be mindful of the evolving nature of technology, and consider reviewing and updating your plans periodically.

Fee Wars

There are fee wars happening with the ETF Investment management firms. Fees are collapsing below 100 basis points, and I believe before it is said and done, we could approach 0% fees. The implication might be to make entering the roach motel of ETFs so attractive that your custody keys will provide the absolute powerhouse of financial bullies, supported by those who hope to keep a good eye on this stack.

Flaws with Bitcoin Custodians

While Bitcoin custodians can provide valuable services in securely storing and managing digital assets, like any system, there are potential flaws and risks associated with custodial solutions.

Custodians add counterparty risk. Custodial solutions involve a level of centralization, as users trust a third party with the custody of their private keys. This introduces a potential single point of failure, and if the custodian is compromised, you are shagged (up the creek without a paddle).

Custodians can go bankrupt, die, face legal issues, flee the jurisdiction, or otherwise fail; thusly users may lose access to their funds. The custodian's financial stability and reputation are crucial considerations.

Custodians, like any online service, may be vulnerable to cyberattacks. If a custodial platform's security measures are insufficient, it could result in the loss or theft of funds.

Custodians often limit users' control over their private keys. Users may not be able to directly access or manage their private keys, limiting their autonomy in particular transactions or circumstances.

Custodial services charge fees for their services, which can include transaction fees, storage fees, or other costs.

Custodians may require users to provide personal information for identity verification and compliance purposes. This raises privacy concerns, especially for those who prioritize maintaining anonymity in their cryptocurrency transactions.

My recommendation, if you don't already know it, is to become knowledgeable and self-custody. I would say the only challenging part is getting a genuinely secure, air-gapped Bitcoin key pair. Buying Bitcoin and sending it to your Bitcoin address is safe and easy. The Bitcoin will grow on its own. You can check on your wealth 24 hours a day, every day, at HTTPS://BLOCKSTREAM.INFO/ or an assortment of other blockchain explorers.

A blockchain explorer is a web-based tool that allows users to view information about transactions, blocks, and addresses on a blockchain network.

Blockstream is a company that focuses on various Bitcoin-related technologies and solutions. The Blockstream Explorer is designed to provide users with a user-friendly interface to explore and analyze activities on the Bitcoin blockchain. Some standard features you might find on a blockchain explorer include:

Transaction details that users can search for and view details about specific Bitcoin transactions, including inputs, outputs, transaction size, fees, and confirmation status.

Block Information: Information about individual blocks are available, including the block height, timestamp, miner, and the list of transactions included in the block.

Users can also explore details about specific Bitcoin addresses, including transaction history, balances, and related addresses.

Network Statistics: Blockstream Explorer provides various statistics related to the Bitcoin network, such as hash rate, difficulty, and other metrics that reflect the network's activity.

Real-Time Transaction Feed: Most explorers offer a real-time feed of new transactions being added to the Bitcoin mempool, waiting to be included in blocks.

View a list of addresses ranked by the amount of Bitcoin they hold, often referred to as a "rich list."

Hardest Money Ever

There is a system that hates Bitcoin; just being there makes the dollar look bad, and for good reason. Bitcoin works perfectly; it is decentralized and permissionless; you don't need permission to do what you want with it. Send a billion dollars' worth from here to China, in less than a second, for less than a dollar. And on and on, but the most significant feature of all is that it is the hardest money ever.

That dollar system includes banks and other financial institutions, the SEC, and anyone vested in trading in the dollar. It's not the weakest money ever, but it is getting there.

Helping Bitcoin

At its core, our government is tied tightly to the dollar via the FED.

The treasury and the FED will do everything in their power to kill Bitcoin while trying to appear to be helping Bitcoin. They will say things like, "*we are here to protect investors*" out of one side of their mouth, while the other side creates extreme volatility, causing havoc by propagandizing that fraudsters swirl only around Bitcoin. They tell us that investors in Bitcoin cannot be protected from fraud, front running, wash sales and other misconduct. They say intermediaries for products that do not comply with federal securities law to register their exchanges worldwide are the problem. They say fraudsters continue to exploit the rising popularity of crypto, in general, but really are thinking about the thorn in their side, Bitcoin. I say if crypto is so popular, why not try to do what is expected of the SEC and create rules and definitions for the marketplace, instead of dragging their feet for the banksters? Even investment firms have been begging for regulatory clarity to no avail. The SEC prefers to teach that they are all powerful and put people in jail for breaking rules that have yet to be written. In conformity with the constitution, it is Congress's job to create laws, not the SEC.

Institutional Investors

$$$ It is impossible for institutional investors to ignore the greatest returning asset of all time. I can guarantee you that they are not here to stick their toe in the water; think more of a cannonball-style entry.

Five billion percent increase.

Coinbase, the San Francisco-based cryptocurrency exchange, announced the launch of a new service called Coinbase International Exchange. The new platform will enable institutional users outside the United States to trade Bitcoin futures. This asset is moving on a fast track with style. OK, maybe a swan dive off an Acapulco high cliff.

Monetary Force Field

There are Forces wanting to protect the U.S. dollar and beneficiaries such as traditional financial institutions, governments, and regulatory bodies that may have concerns or reservations about the rise of Bitcoin. The reasons for this are multifaceted. Central banks and governments generally prefer to maintain control over any monetary force field. The decentralized and borderless nature of Bitcoin challenges this control.

Bitcoin is a threat and is automatically viewed as a competitor to traditional fiat currencies. If Bitcoin gains widespread adoption, it will impact and diminish the value of fiat currencies, especially the U.S. dollar.

Regulatory bodies are the strong arm of central banks. Neither of these are Bitcoin's friends. The decentralized nature of Bitcoin can be seen as a direct threat to traditional financial institutions, as it introduces powerful alternatives to conventional banking systems.

In all the effort made to staunchly guard their pile of dollars by denigrating Bitcoin repeatedly, Bitcoin moves forward, tick-tock-next-block. The slope is getting steeper and more slippery,

I encourage you to tune out the negative press and get on board. Up 5 billion percent. I hear people say, "I missed the train." Yes, you missed the first five billion percent. But, the party has really just started.

Unprecedented Expansion

$$$ The spot Bitcoin Exchange Traded Fund ETF is promising. It could solidify an unprecedented expansion of the Bitcoin market.   The integration of such an ETF within 401(k) plans and pensions could be a noteworthy disruptor. This unlocks Bitcoin exposure for mainstream retirement savers.   Moreover channeling a portion of the $8 trillion assets under management (AUM) into 401(k) plans into Bitcoin. This is based on the approval of a spot Bitcoin ETF, which would mark a milestone transition into the accessibility of Bitcoin as an investment class.   By including a spot Bitcoin ETF in 401(k), companies would offer their employees a regulated and familiar way to invest in Bitcoin. This would lower the bar to entry for retirement savers persuaded of Bitcoin's undeveloped promise.

10X Global

$$$ With Bitcoin, there are almost 12 orders of magnitude in market capitalization developed over a period of as many years. In the next order of magnitude, the Bitcoin market cap will move from 1 trillion to 10 trillion. This may not happen in the next year, but it will happen. This translates to a Bitcoin price nearing half a million dollars per Bitcoin.

Bitcoin is on track to take over not only the dollar but all failing currencies, repricing the bond market, the derivatives market, all real estate, gold, and all wealth as a store of value. This will take time, but I prefer to invest in an issue rising in orders of magnitude. Look at the history and do the math... Over five billion percent increase!

As a reference point, in 2020, Bitcoin rose from 18k to 69K, with only 15 billion of inflow.

Today, the on-exchange Bitcoin holds fewer Bitcoins than in 2020. This alone can cause a sharp spike in the price of Bitcoin, even in orders of magnitude higher. **Any number of entities could swamp the market and evaporate the exchange of Bitcoin as a god candle runs, looking for any seller, much like a stock short squeeze on steroids for an extended period.** Frankly, I experienced this very thing, wondering when any bid would catch hold back in 2017. The pressure today is exponentially higher. If it weren't for trumped-up news stories putting individuals in jail for life, Bitcoin would be far, far higher today. The institutions are trying to get a foothold on the biggest stacks of Sats they can by conspiring to create regulatory FUD. I tell you now that they cannot control Bitcoin, and they can barely hinder it.

Conspiracy Theory

The U.S. government may come into possession of Bitcoin through various means, such as asset forfeitures, legal cases, or other circumstances. However, the details of government-held Bitcoin are not routinely disclosed to the public.

Sometimes, I think the whole system has decided the dollar game is kaput. And the chess match is on. How would they approach collecting Bitcoin with all their might? With all their deception? With their printing press? I suppose that it could be a coordinated assault on the order book during tragic news. Orson Welles's adaptation of The *"War of the Worlds"* was performed and broadcast live on October 30, 1938, over the CBS Radio Network. The episode is famous for inciting panic by convincing some members of the listening audience that a Martian invasion was taking place. The episode is famous for inciting panic by convincing some members of the listening audience that a Martian invasion was taking place. Are Manipulators using this tactic?

If anyone has any input on this front, don't hesitate to get in touch with me. I feel like a deer in the headlights trying to figure this one out.

Vested Sovereigns

Small and mid-sized countries are contemplating Bitcoin purchases in the range of a $700 billion investment. More dramatic sovereign Bitcoin acceptance is on the way; including countries such as El Salvador, Argentina, and a handful of African countries. Some rumblings in Germany will also lead to dramatic shifts to hard money. This, as fiat makes daily headlines on every level viral, begets viral against fiat and towards hard money.

The Distant Truth

This is speculation, but truth be told, I think Bitcoin will eventually be colored, not by Bitcoin's effectiveness but by a twisting of the concepts in the minds of the consensus. Bitcoin ETF is a twisted start. If and when the consensus allows for contortions, it will be a much more seasoned Bitcoin quite a distance from here, closer to maturity. The form it will take, will be something like allowing for a centralization. Face it, we are all the same and situated in our hearts; we all long to worship a "king" so that we can cast blame on him rather than ourselves.

Bitcoin is an adolescent and will run for decades before the manipulators gain any foothold. It is abundantly clear to me that the only alternative is to continue to use dollars or a more dystopian form of them, to completely enslave everyone. This book is your heads up.

What can Anyone Do?

A simple approach is to buy Bitcoin hard now and HODL. Then, resist onboarding of social media manipulation techniques. Put on the armor against the manipulator's propaganda operations through Bitcoin education.

Enjoy life and wait to buy your dream house. You may hear from the proverbial shoeshine boy; for the sake of argument, one or two million dollars per Bitcoin then convert half to physical gold or silver and splurge a little.

Better yet, borrow against the Bitcoin and use the interest as a write-off. I will not expound on it here, but DeFi lending institutions will happily use multi-sig private keys to securely collateralize your Bitcoin without risk to them or your Bitcoin.

Get started now for zero cost by setting up an account with https://www.swanbitcoin.com/ or https://unchained.com/. I have no interest in promoting these except that, for now, they foster the right culture and education. Pull the trigger when you are convinced to do so.

It is a difficult job keeping track of most of the players and their motives, but frankly, if you were to get Bitcoin now and just HODL, that would be all there was to it. And live happily. I find it weird talking about risk tolerance here, as where is the risk? Is the risk of purchasing Bitcoin as the hardest money in the world? Or, is it in holding dollars and related dollar-denominated assets?

We live in a world where we ostensibly vote for politicians who make regulations and laws to protect investors and their money from a system designed to steal it. This is precisely why the government grows year in and year out; who in turn offers us a carrot on a stick granting the possibility of more stimulus or free student loans, or Universal Basic Income or, or, or... Money will not break; it is already broken. We are just unaware of it or have clearly not defined "broken money."

I believe you need to make a choice. That choice is what percentage of your investment portfolio do you allocate to Bitcoin: 1%, 10%, 50%, or 100%.

I suppose it really hinges on your education level rather than your normalcy bias in dollars.

Just Do It

Buy $100 of Bitcoin regardless of the price or your education.

Securely obtain a paper wallet (created by an air-gapped computer) shown in this book.

Place your PK (private key) in 2 or 3 secure locations, and do not reveal your PK to anyone.

Forget about this investment, but don't stop learning.

Do not give in to FUD (fear, uncertainty and doubt).

Let me put it another way. If you are a teenager or a centenarian and you read through my book two or three times; you could scrape together four or five thousand dollars to buy 0.1 Bitcoin. Then you could sock it away, and wait for a one million dollar print in a year or two and retire comfortably when everyone else is scrambling around trying to hold it together with disintegrating dollars. Anyone can do it with 10 hours of education on YouTube.

The Marginal Cost of Production

The marginal cost of production is a concept in economics that refers to the additional cost incurred by producing one more unit of a good or service. The concept of marginal cost is essential for businesses to make production-level decisions. It helps determine whether it is economically beneficial to monitor the increase or decrease of production. In a perfectly competitive market, companies generally aim to produce where marginal cost equals the market price to maximize profit. This, by itself, leads directly to deflation. The buyer is the other half of the deflationary equation, always wanting less expensive prices.

The marginal cost of production is the cost incurred for each extra output produced, only incrementally cheaper. With Bitcoin, a line of code is inexpensive. A line of code written by a line of code (AI) is cheaper yet. This brings the marginal cost of production very close to zero.

The use of Bitcoin, which is basically trustless, is produced from secure lines of code; the more they are adopted, the more secure and efficient they become. This is based on proof of work, which is expanding daily and is more efficient in the same vein.

Bitcoin is fixed, trustworthy, and transparent. There is no CEO to arrest or central point of authority to pressure. Bitcoin can eliminate monetary and debt inflation. The only one responsible for it now is you.

Bitcoin's only vulnerability is the manipulator's ability to coerce the consensus and simultaneously shoot themselves in the foot to their detriment. This is not something wrong with Bitcoin but with people's hearts. Currently, we all live in a controlled collectivist hive mind using and believing in broken money without a single vote; well, not one that matters anyway. Did you get to vote on how much money is manipulated or inflated? Unless you are Jerome Powel or Janet Yellen, I think not. Bitcoin fixes that with an automatic discipline, and you get a powerful vote. "Yes, you can" continue to vote for a broken money system if that is what you wish. Or you can vote for Bitcoin. Don't vote for the lesser of two evils; vote for individual sovereignty.

Bitcoin Counterculture

How do you think the Bitcoin counterculture label was applied? Psychological operations (PSYOPS) are operations to convey selected information and indicators to audiences to influence their motives and the behavior of governments, organizations, and groups. Hundreds-of-millions were poured into protecting the dollar's hegemony and power. A five hundred trillion-dollar business based on US treasuries; this will be next to be fractionalized and sold in an ETF format. These fractionalized treasuries, which will be the wizard-conjured basis of the world's love affair with a lie, are pumped into managed assets everywhere. This will be the exact mechanism used to wrap a Bitcoin in an ETF, sell it as Bitcoin, and centralize it in the process. Bitcoin will win that war but people's perception of Bitcoin will take a beating if they keep piling into the ETF.

The SEC will constantly try to corral all exchanges either by rabid enforcement or forced regulation compliance in an attempt to close on and off ramps. Ultimately, this will fail, and even the manipulators will fall into the "if we can't beat them, join them" attitude.

Bitcoin has been poking and prodding attack vectors from every direction to no avail. Proof of work was offered up to the (ESG) **environmental, social, and governance** crowd. It was proven that Bitcoin provided, through the use of stranded energy, the ability to encourage better and more efficient power production plants, especially in impoverished nations. Now, these nations can become productive and contribute to the world's efficient output; "a mind is a terrible thing to waste." Bitcoin mining is focusing more on renewables. Elitist, in their woke condition, fosters this wasted energy and water FUD; in hopes that some of their crap will stick. People harbor jealousy even when the poorest of the poor find some element of comfort or empowerment.

The real triumph would be the transition from clinging to fiat to belief in hard money, Bitcoin. Follow the rulers or simply follow the rules.

Unfortunately, most Americans are susceptible to the temptation of free money, UBI (Universal Basic Income), welfare, stimulus money, reparations, EIC (Earned Income Credits), free money for states, assistance programs, American Rescue Plan Act, Federal Funding Opportunities, continuous commercials for free money and the list goes on and on. This in exchange for our willingness to bow down to this government god and by extension worship the power of the printing presses continuous QE.

This continued misplaced faith will subjectively destroy us and everything else it touches. Because we all need to live, eat, and sleep, *my favorite is air conditioning*; our default is dollars, which we all support without a vote. With Bitcoin, you vote with your feet by how much fiat is converted and placed in an honest ledger with unchanging rules and magnificent appreciation.

Skills, hard work and talent are ubiquitous worldwide.

Thus, people will race to it, especially as the manipulators attempt to sanction it.

Most cannot predict appropriately because they need to think from their first true principles or the true natural next step. This is hard, and people are naturally lazy and covet convenience. Generally, they want to be a little better off than their neighbor or, at minimum, keep up with the Joneses.

$$$ Today, as fiat prints faster and faster, more people will move to Bitcoin. This is just a fact.

I feel a rant coming on...

The world works harder and harder for less and less when it should be the other way around. Like buying a television, each year, TVs get better and better and cheaper and cheaper. Obviously, the system's motive for this is to keep us glued and watching their PROGRAMING! It used to be that a one-wage earner could have a family and a lovely home. Now, it's not so easy even with two wage earners in the family. The fact is the dollar is already the walking dead. The Fed knows it, the banks know it, Hunter Biden knows it. Debase it, abuse it, give it away, authorize $5 million reparations; it does not matter. The only reason you are taxed any longer is to provide a carrot on a stick, to keep you in a state of suspended animation until it is worth less and less, eventually, depending on your willingness to be enslaved, worthless!

Bitcoin was discovered in 2008. Not an invention. I do not take anything away from the efforts of the people who prepared the protocol built around Bitcoin. Cryptographic technology fixes money in every way. They are nerd heroes who deserve "fat stacks."

How could regulation through institutions based on a system built on theft, corruption, inflation, and onerous taxation even work? I can only surmise that it was the frog in the warming bath.

The Internet is ubiquitous. Can you remember the last budding Internet conference? In an attempt to show the maturity or immaturity of Bitcoin, we are just now moving onto the Bitcoin stage! And the show must go on.

Twenty-one million fixed pegged Bitcoin vs. QE; study the long-term parabolic chart starting in 2009.

The First Published Exchange Rate

The first known published Bitcoin exchange rate to US dollars occurred on October 5, 2009. The first recorded Bitcoin exchange rate was established on the now-famous BitcoinMarket.com, a platform created by software developer, Jed McCaleb. The initial price was set at 1,309.03 Bitcoins for one 1 US dollar.

In the early days of Bitcoin, the value was not established through a traditional exchange or market but rather through direct user agreements. BitcoinMarket.com played a role by providing a platform where users could post bids and offers, helping to create a more organized and accessible marketplace for Bitcoin trading.

Bitcoin to USD exchange rate has experienced significant changes, with the value of Bitcoin undergoing substantial growth and volatility over the years. The cryptocurrency's price discovery is now facilitated by numerous exchanges worldwide, each determining its own Bitcoin to USD exchange rate based on market supply and demand.

How much has Bitcoin appreciated since its first published price?

Bitcoin's first recorded price is often considered to be 10,000 Bitcoin for two pizzas, which were exchanged in May, 2010. The transaction is known as "Bitcoin Pizza Day," and it established a benchmark for valuing Bitcoin in a real-world transaction. At that time, the value of 10,000 Bitcoin was approximately $41.

To calculate the percent gain from the first published exchange rate of 1300 Bitcoin to 1 dollar to today's exchange rate of $44,000 to 1 Bitcoin, you can use the following formula:

Percent Gain=(Final Value−Initial ValueInitial Value)×100Percent Gain=(Initial ValueFinal Value−Initial Value)×100

In this formula:

"Final Value" is the current value of Bitcoin, which is $44,000.

"Initial Value" is the value of Bitcoin at its first published exchange rate to dollars, which is 1300 Bitcoin to 1 dollar.

Substitute these values into the formula:

Percent Gain=(44,000−1130011300)×100Percent Gain=(1300144,000−13001)×100

Calculate the numerator and denominator separately:

Percent Gain=(43,999.999230811300)×100Percent Gain=(1300143,999.9992308)×100

Now, perform the division:

Percent Gain≈5,384,614,517.58%Percent Gain≈5,384,614,517.58%

So, the percent gain from the initial exchange rate of 1300 Bitcoin to 1 dollar to the current exchange rate of $44,000 to 1 Bitcoin is approximately 5,384,614,517.58%.

Bitcoin is Good Money

First, Bitcoin is good money. All other cryptocurrencies are foolish copies of Bitcoin. I'm not saying you can't make money with shitcoins (excuse my French). I am saying shitcoins have a fiat aspect to them, and you will eventually lose your shirt.

Bitcoin will go viral and infect the whole world with its value proposition. Some of those values are as follows:

A trustless money

Permissionless money

Decentralized money

Censorship resistant

Unconfiscatable (if properly stored) even under duress

Demands a flight to quality

Not inflationary (fixed 21 million)

Good money stores financial energy. You work to create order and, in return, receive a paycheck that you can spend. But, you might keep some of it for a rainy day in a traditional bank that offers you 0.1% interest, which, after tax, bank bail-ins, taxman clawbacks, garnishments, and lawsuits, assuming you are not judgment-proof, leaves you a good reason not to save in a bank. The same applies to an IRA, dollar-denominated bond, stock, or other investment vehicles.

Money evolves naturally. Whether it be beads, shells, barter bucks, gold, or even early bank currency, originally, these were all inherently decentralized money. In their desire to control and then unnaturally centralize it, governments are currently doing so through banksters and Federal Reserve regulators.

I like to take note of people's patterns. Gary Gensler, Elizabeth Warren, Jamie Dimon, Xi, Christen LaGard... you continue the list. All these openly despise Bitcoin because they are all vested in dollar control. And they all promise to fix things for you if only you would continue to trust them.

I suggest you take a moment to consider where to best place your trust. Do these Bitcoin despisers deserve your monetary trust?

Another thing to ponder is how much trust you place in the dollar. FYI, dollars are no longer backed by gold or anything since Richard Nixon closed the gold window in 1971. The Constitution does not support dollars. Article IV, Section 1 states that Full Faith and Credit shall be given to the public Acts in each State.

Honestly, they do not deserve our trust. And the only full faith they refer to has been twisted into "our" faith in their dollar regardless of how much they debauch it. Ever since the Garden of Eden, it almost seems that we have come to depend on tyranny.

The Fly in the Ointment

First, Bitcoin is not an invention. It is a perfect structure built on math, set in an expanding network, discovered by **"Satoshi Nakamoto."** Try to understand this system is flawless; it works perfectly and cannot be corrupted, as it is simply math. Tried and true using an open-source code. What can be corrupted is the perception of the system of Bitcoin; the twisting of words and definitions.

For example, elements of the tenets of Bitcoin can be pecked at. The associated assumptions, such as Bitcoin being decentralized, will be diminished with the application of the Bitcoin spot ETF being considered actual Bitcoin.

Unlike the previous *"futures Bitcoin ETFs,"* which were connected by index only future contracts or shares of Bitcoin-related companies; these new spot Bitcoin ETFs funds, through a ticket called *"a create,"* hold Bitcoins via a custodian. These ETFs should closely track the spot price of Bitcoin long term, all without acknowledging the true values of the underlying asset, the promise of owning your own money, instead of just having access to your funds.

A spot Bitcoin ETF is a regulated way of owning an index to Bitcoin. It is not owning Bitcoin. Again, this is another opportunity to say, "Not your keys, not your Bitcoin." A firm such as BlackRock or Coinbase holds keys to Bitcoin, which, in turn, provides you with a contract that does a good job paralleling the price of Bitcoin. Quite honestly, the devil is in the details of that ETF contract, much akin to the difference between physical and paper gold. You are not going to end up with Bitcoin or its glorious features. BlackRock will end up owning millions of Bitcoin in custody storage. Now, what they do with that honeypot in time is anybody's guess. This is one possible example of centralization.

There is no externally imposed Bitcoin inflation. But, there are thousands of copycat cryptocurrencies for Bitcoin to contend with, most of which have little or no use cases. All of these copycat cryptocurrencies are an attempt at temporary inflation. These cryptocurrencies are dying and will, for the most part, evaporate in time. As they evaporate, the capital will move back to Bitcoin. Again, this vindication and reallocating of capital is not a Bitcoin error but merely a perspective error. If you are not following me here, just don't buy "shitcoins"!

The true use case of Bitcoin is not as a cryptocurrency as most people believe; it is a store of wealth. As a matter of course, I do not refer to Bitcoin as a cryptocurrency because the manipulators comingled those terms, specifically so Bitcoin would necessarily need to compete as a cryptocurrency. I purposely keep the two terms separate. Mixing them together is done intentionally to make it confusing. There is no shit attached to Bitcoin. There is Bitcoin, and there are cryptocurrency shitcoins.

They are not one and the same. Bitcoin will emerge as a perfect reserve asset, whereby you can store money in a very secure environment until you need to use it. On the other hand, "shitcoins" are, for lack of a better term, shit. Many newbie Bitcoiners will not get this distinction and end up losing Bitcoin in the process.

Time to Spend:

When you make that first Bitcoin investment, don't spend it all. When it has matured to your satisfaction, then at this point, you might use the Lightning Network or some HD wallet to transfer from your "Bitcoin reserve bank" to your preferred spending wallet. Perfectly held reserve currency is the future of Bitcoins use case.

Again, don't spend your "hardest money in the world" borrow against it. In the meantime, spend all of your fiat with abandon!   Whatever you do, don't convert the hardest money into termite-ridden cash.

MOFO FOMO

$$$ Yes, Fear Of Missing Out (FOMO) is a powerful psychological phenomenon that can influence people to buy Bitcoin. FOMO occurs when individuals see others making profits or participating in a trend and fear that they will miss out on potential gains. This fear can drive impulsive buying decisions as individuals rush to join the market to avoid being left behind, typically without

accompanying knowledge or due diligence. Some, if not all, of these FOMO investors, accidentally benefit, because of the lack of education, FUD (Fear, Uncertainty, and Doubt) is produced, leading to selling your hardest money in exchange for broken money. Both FOMO and FUD are emotional. In comparison, education produces confidence and eventually, freedom.

The price surges with Bitcoin experiences can be rapid price increases, especially during bull markets, FOMO tends to intensify as people fear missing out on these profits.

Positive media coverage, especially stories of individuals making significant profits from Bitcoin investments, contributes further to FOMO. Positive narratives can create a potent sense of urgency to buy before prices rise even further, and further. This has been going on for the entire life of Bitcoin. My take on this phenomenon is that people use their gut understanding of Bitcoin rather than their head knowledge. This comes from a fear that it might be too difficult for them to understand. I am here to assure you it is not.

Social media platforms play a significant role in spreading information and trends—posts about rising Bitcoin prices, success stories, and a general sense of excitement. The combination of honest working Bitcoin and the viral effect can trigger FOMO among followers.

Down the Rabbit Hole

The term "going down the rabbit hole" is often used in the context of Bitcoin to describe the process of deepening one's understanding and involvement in the Bitcoin space. It suggests a journey of increasing curiosity, exploration, and engagement with various aspects of Bitcoin, adding to a broader knowledge of Bitcoin technology.

Individuals often enter cryptocurrency by hearing about Bitcoin from friends, media, or online sources. They may be attracted to the idea of decentralized digital currency and the potential for financial gains. After learning about Bitcoin, they might make their first purchase to experiment with and better understand how transactions work.

Falling down the rabbit hole often involves delving into the underlying technology of Bitcoin and blockchain technology. Enthusiasts may start learning about decentralized ledgers, consensus mechanisms, and the principles that make blockchain secure and transparent.

As individuals become even more involved, they may explore various aspects of Bitcoin, such as its history, development, and the philosophy behind it. This stage often involves reading books, articles, and whitepapers to gain a deeper understanding like you are doing now.

Many people jump down the rabbit hole by actively participating in online forums, social media, and local meetups. Engaging with the broader Bitcoin community provides opportunities to share ideas, discuss developments, and learn from others.

Some of those people develop a firm conviction in the principles of decentralization, censorship resistance, and financial sovereignty promoted by Bitcoin. This should lead to a long-term commitment to Bitcoin and its quintessential precepts.

Individuals who have fallen deep down the rabbit hole eventually contribute to the Bitcoin ecosystem in various ways. This could include development contributions, educational initiatives, or advocating for an even wider adoption.

Bitcoin Absorbs All of the World's Wealth

The short answer is yes, it can. The longer answer is yes, it will. Referring back to Gresham's law, it took ten years (1963-1973) for the lion's share of silver coins to be hoarded. Now that Bitcoin is recognized as an asset class, I do not give it three years to disappear from exchanges, 2023-2026, it will disappear as silver did from our currency. Bitcoin here is the hardest money in the world.

$$$ The idea that Bitcoin absorbs all of the world's wealth is an interesting proposition and a worthy thought process. We need to consider when exploring this, if Bitcoin absorbs all of the world's wealth, the market capitalization would need to surpass the total value of all

global assets, including gold, but not paper gold, real estate, stocks, bonds, other precious metals, art, and more—approximately a 700 trillion dollar equivalent.

Global wealth distribution would require a significant restructuring of the entire global economic system. This is already happening right now.

Bitcoin is known for its price volatility. It would need to stabilize significantly to become a global store of value or means of exchange. Without exterior meddling and as the price increases, volatility will be diminished.

Competition with Other Assets:

Overcoming significant inertia in transitioning individuals' and institutions' wealth to Bitcoin will take time, but it will happen all the same.

The evolution of technology, financial instruments, and economic systems is fluid and dynamic. Bitcoin and its adaptations to traditional finance will impact finance for decades to come.

The Depth of the Bitcoin Market

The depth of the Bitcoin market refers to the level of liquidity and the order book of buy and sell orders at various price levels. It shows how much trading activity is present at different prices. The order book typically consists of two sides:

The bid side represents the buyer's desire to buy. It shows the quantity of Bitcoin buyers are willing to purchase at various price levels. The ask side represents the seller's interest in selling at different price levels.

The depth of the market is often visualized in a chart known as the "order book depth chart." This chart displays the cumulative order quantities at each price level, helping traders and investors gauge the market's potential support and resistance levels.

A deep market with significant buy and sell orders at various prices may indicate a more liquid and stable market, making it easier for traders to execute trades without causing considerable price fluctuations. On the other hand, a shallow market with fewer orders may be more susceptible to rapid price movements.

If the depth of the Bitcoin market shows many bids with almost no asks, it suggests a scenario with a strong demand from buyers (bids) and limited supply from sellers (asks). In this situation, the price would increase substantially. The high demand for Bitcoin (represented by the high bids) and the limited supply (low asks) could significantly enlarge the Bitcoin price. With more buyers looking to purchase and fewer sellers willing to sell, the natural market forces would escalate the price upward until the price reached willing sellers. Remember, the willing seller metric is currently at an all-time high and moving only in one direction. HODLers heaven! Bear in mind, currently, 71% of Bitcoin is HODLed, up substantially from all years before. These Bitcoin are not traded but in strong hands. The longer people hold Bitcoin, the further down the rabbit hole they go. We should consider the coming ETF and how many buyers are coming. This on top of a naturally shrinking supply (the halving); with the lack of sell orders (asks) resulting in fewer sellers in the market; a large buy order could cause an enormous price spike, especially when there is not enough supply to meet that demand. This can lead to rapid and astronomical price movements, known as a god candles. Then comes the proverbial "to the moon Alice" scenario ensuing.

Exchange-Traded Fund

The likelihood that investors in a Bitcoin spot exchange-traded fund (ETF) would move to the underlying Bitcoin asset depends on convenience and accessibility. Still, in the meantime, they support the upward price action, and I admit as much as I disdain the spot ETF, I will enjoy the constant and guaranteed long-term price increase.

If these investors later decide they want direct ownership of Bitcoin or prefer the features of holding the underlying asset, they may choose to transition to holding actual Bitcoins. Market conditions and the performance of Bitcoin can influence investor decisions. Suppose Bitcoin experiences significant price appreciation or becomes more widely accepted. In that case, investors may be more inclined to hold the actual asset to benefit from direct potential gains without fees or government confiscation and seizure burn.

The structure and costs associated with the ETF can play a temporary role. Investors might evaluate factors such as fees, tax implications, and even the ease of buying and selling the ETF compared to acquiring and self-custody of actual Bitcoin.

Do Not Reveal Your Private Keys

Should you decide to self-custody, how you handle your private key is the quintessential essence of your financial security. You wouldn't leave your purse or wallet full of cash on the sidewalk overnight, so keep your private keys safe from prying eyes, especially Internet eyes.

Conveying the importance of not exposing private keys is crucial in promoting security and protecting individuals from potential financial losses.

Securing your Bitcoin holdings involves implementing several best practices to protect your private keys and maintain the integrity of your assets. Here are some essential security best practices for handling Bitcoin.

The use of a hardware wallet such as a Trezor for storing your Bitcoin offline is good. Hardware wallets are offline devices that provide enhanced security by keeping your private keys offline, away from potential online threats. Almost everyone encourages this as a safe practice. I like simple, easy-to-understand methods. It would take me a long time to deconstruct the code in any hardware wallet and endorse it with my trust. I have said it before and say it again throughout this book: obtain an air-gapped paper wallet; and long-term store this cold wallet offline. **(completely safe)** These are easy to understand wallets. You could store a thousand of them in varying Bitcoin denominations, awaiting the day you want to take one wallet and spend it or place it into a hardware wallet to spend. It is safe and easy to load your paper wallet from any Bitcoin exchange or peer-to-peer with the address side of your key pair. Show this address side of your key pair to the world. The worst thing they can do to the address side is fund your Bitcoin wallet.

Secure Your Private Keys:

Never share your private keys with anyone. This is the completely private side of your key pair. Keep them offline and store them in a secure location. Do not store your private keys on easily accessible devices or in the cloud. They will vanish along with your funds.

Enable Two-Factor Authentication (2FA) if you are not using paper wallets. There is no need for paper wallets to be exposed online, assuming you obtained them with an air-gapped protocol.

Enable 2FA on any accounts or platforms associated with your Bitcoin hot wallet and keep only funds you plan on spending for that day or week. This adds an extra layer of security by requiring a second form of verification beyond your password.

Update Software Regularly. Again, there is no need to update with paper wallets.

Keep your hot wallet software, operating system, and antivirus programs up to date.

Use Strong Passwords:

Choose strong, unique passwords for your wallet, exchange accounts, and any other platforms related to your Bitcoin holdings. Consider using a password manager to generate and store complex passwords related to your hot wallets. These steps are unrelated to your paper wallet's private key.

Be Cautious with Online Storage:

Please stay away from online wallets and be cautious about any security measures they have in place. You absolutely must choose reputable platforms with a track record of security and use additional security features, if available, such as 2FA.

Verify Transactions:

When making a purchase or receiving Bitcoin, confirm any and all Bitcoin transactions and carefully review the details to ensure accuracy. Confirm that the recipient's address, amount, and any transaction fees are correct to prevent accidental or malicious transactions.

Educate Yourself:

Stay informed about common security threats and scams related to Bitcoin. Be cautious of phishing attempts, fake wallets, and fraudulent schemes. Verifying Bitcoin is easy and completely safe. You can view any transactions, present and past. You can view these transactions day or night on many Bitcoin explorers, such as:

https://www.blockchain.com/explorer

Backup your Wallet:

Back up your wallets seed phrase or private keys in at least two secure locations. This ensures that you can recover your funds if your device is lost, stolen, or damaged.

Practice Cold Storage:

Use cold storage solutions, such as hardware wallets offline or paper wallets, for long-term storage of significant amounts of Bitcoin. Cold storage keeps private keys entirely offline, eliminating the risk of online vulnerabilities.

Protect Personal Information

Be cautious about sharing personal information online, especially information related to your Bitcoin holdings. Avoid discussing your holdings on public forums or social media.

Except to say, "Unfortunately, I lost all my Bitcoin in a terrible boating accident."

Test Transactions with Small Amounts:

When using a new wallet or making significant changes, test transactions with small amounts to ensure everything works as expected before transferring more substantial sums.

By implementing these security best practices, you can significantly reduce the risk of unauthorized access, theft, or loss of your Bitcoin holdings. It's crucial to stay vigilant and adapt to evolving security threats in the Bitcoin space.

My recommended choice is to use a cold storage paper wallet, which is not online and is easily understood. Paper wallets should be created by a technique called air gapping. Paper wallets, once created and funded, require extra steps to spend. Bitcoin should be purchased and vaulted until you completely understand the spending mechanism.

Information regarding air-gapped wallets can be found at the following address: WWW.BITCOINMOUTH.COM

Fixed Supply

The fixed supply of Bitcoin at 21 million coins contrasts sharply with the concept of quantitative easing (QE), which is a monetary policy tool used by central banks to increase the money supply.

Bitcoin was designed with a capped supply of 21 million coins by its creator, **Satoshi Nakamoto**. This fixed supply is encoded into the Bitcoin protocol, forming a fundamental aspect of Bitcoin's monetary policy. The fixed supply is intended to mimic the scarcity and divisibility of precious metals like gold only in a superior manner.

QE is a monetary policy tool used by central banks to stimulate the economy. It involves the central bank purchasing financial assets, typically government bonds, with the goal of injecting money into the economy. The increase in the money supply is intended to encourage spending and investment during times of economic downturns.

QE contributes to the expansion of the money supply, leading to inflationary pressure in fiat currencies. By increasing the supply of money, central banks aim to influence interest rates and economic activity. However, sustained QE can raise concerns about potential long-term effects on inflation and a currency's purchasing power.

In summary, Bitcoin's fixed supply of 21 million coins sets it apart from traditional fiat currencies, which can experience fluctuations in supply due to central bank policies like QE. Bitcoin's scarcity and hands-off policy have contributed to its appeal as a digital asset and superior store of value. Even though the dollar is the cleanest shirt in the hamper, compared to other world currencies, it still degrades annually at seven and a half percent annually on average. This directly steals money right from your rear hip pocket every day.

Bitcoin Maturity

$$$ Candidates for Congress, Senate, and President are stumping for and promoting Bitcoin now, as it matures.

Determining Bitcoin's exact "maturity" on a timeline depends on the specific aspects you're considering. Since its creation in 2009, Bitcoin has evolved through various phases, and different observers may have different perspectives on its development. Here are some key milestones and stages in Bitcoin's maturity.

The nascent years 2009-2012:

Bitcoin's early years were characterized by its creation and the establishment of the first decentralized blockchain. During this period, Bitcoin gained attention primarily among enthusiasts and early adopters.

Early Growth 2013-2017:

Bitcoin's price experienced significant volatility during this period, reaching new highs and gaining increased public attention. Infrastructure and services around Bitcoin, such as exchanges and wallets, also started to develop. The market cap and ecosystem expanded, attracting more mainstream interest.

Next:

Institutional Interest 2018- to present date, and growing exponentially.

Next Stage:

Regulatory developments have contributed to Bitcoin's maturity. Different countries have approached Bitcoin regulation differently, and ongoing regulatory discussions continue to shape the landscape.

Next Stage:

Bitcoin's infrastructure has continued to mature with the development of improved wallets, exchanges, and custody solutions. Additionally, the integration of Bitcoin into mainstream financial services has been progressing, with more businesses accepting Bitcoin as a form of payment naturally since it is the best form of money in the world.

Next Stage:

Bitcoin is often referred to as "digital gold" due to its perceived store of value characteristics. This narrative has gained traction, with Bitcoin being positioned as a potential long-term answer to economic uncertainty.

Growing institutional adoption occurred in the early 2020s, with major companies and financial institutions expressing interest in Bitcoin. Still, very few institutions have added Bitcoin to their balance sheets without FASB accounting, which should gain traction towards the end of 2024.

Bitcoin is still in the early stages of development with the backdrop of enveloping all wealth. At the same time, Bitcoin is an established asset class still in the early stages of development. This provides a powerful opportunity to escape fiat.

On the S Curve

The "S-curve" concept is often used to describe the adoption and diffusion of new technologies. In the context of Bitcoin, the S-curve represents the growth of adoption over time.

Here's a general breakdown of the S-curve stages and a discussion on where some observers believe Bitcoin might be.

Bitcoin started in the innovation stage, where it was primarily known and used by technology enthusiasts, cypherpunks, and early adopters. During this phase, the technology was experimental, and its use was extremely limited. Few were aware of its robust potential.

Bitcoin has moved beyond the innovation stage and is currently in the early adoption stage. More individuals, institutions, and businesses have become aware of and started to adopt Bitcoin. This phase involves increasing interest, investment, and integration into the financial ecosystem.

Soon, we will be getting ready to enter the early majority stage with the coming of the Bitcoin ETF, which would involve a more significant wave of mainstream adoption spanning the next four or five years. This extreme running of the bulls pushes the price of Bitcoin to unbelievable heights, especially as infrastructure develops and institutions become more comfortable with Bitcoin. I might change the name to a Tyrannosaurus-rex market rather than a bull market.

Review https://bitcointreasuries.net to see the hard numbers of various entities that hold Bitcoin.

Required Layers

Bitcoin operates within a layered technology stack that relies on various components, each playing a crucial role in its functionality and adoption. Below are the essential layers.

The physical infrastructure layer involves the hardware and network infrastructure that supports the operation of the Bitcoin network. This includes mining hardware (ASICs), data centers, and the global network of nodes that validate and relay already operational transactions.

The Internet is a fundamental layer for Bitcoin's operation. It provides the communication infrastructure through which nodes in the network can connect and exchange information. The decentralized and global nature of the Internet is essential for the peer-to-peer nature of Bitcoin transactions. The blockchain protocol layer is the core technology of Bitcoin and already works perfectly on the Internet; the Internet took years to morph into what it is today, a universal, everyday tool for most; what a fortunate stroke of luck. Bitcoin absolutely needs the Internet.

Bitcoin instantly dovetailed into the Internet protocol and has very few demands of it, allowing it to grow and flourish.

The blockchain protocol layer includes the consensus rules, cryptographic algorithms, and the structure of the blockchain itself. Bitcoin's blockchain is a distributed ledger that records all transactions in a secure and transparent manner.

The mining and consensus layer involves the process of adding transactions to the blockchain. Miners use computational power to solve complex mathematical problems, and the consensus algorithm (Proof-of-Work in Bitcoin's case) ensures that all nodes agree on the state of the blockchain.

The network layer facilitates the communication between nodes in the Bitcoin network. Nodes share information about transactions, blocks, and the overall state of the blockchain. The peer-to-peer networks provide for the decentralized nature of the system.

The wallet and user interface layer allows tools and applications for users to interact with the Bitcoin network. This includes software and hardware wallets, and paper wallets as well as user interfaces for making transactions, checking balances, and managing private keys.

Security is a critical aspect of the Bitcoin ecosystem. This layer involves mechanisms such as cryptographic algorithms, private key management, and best practices for securing transactions and funds. Security measures ensure the integrity and confidentiality of user transactions.

The financial infrastructure layer encompasses various services and institutions that facilitate the exchange of Bitcoin for fiat currencies and other assets. This includes exchanges, over-the-counter (OTC) platforms, and other financial institutions that provide on-ramps and off-ramps to the traditional financial system. These happen very naturally without the need for regulatory oversight. The good would remain, and the bad actors would naturally vanish. Someday, there will be no further need for exchanges as Bitcoin may not care to trade with dollars or any other fiat. Automated atomic swaps may exchange Bitcoin, for example, ETH, or a comparable currency. This would leave no further whipping boys for the SEC to punish and create FUD.

Each of these layers is interconnected, and Bitcoin's success and adoption depend on the robustness and collaboration of the entire ecosystem. The layers collectively contribute to the Bitcoin network's permissionless nature. It's worth noting that the development of each layer is constantly improving in speed and efficiency.

Dollar Cognitive Dissonance

How have advanced functionality and the adoption of Bitcoin overcome the cognitive dissonance emanating from the standpoint of registered investment advisers (RIA) and institutions whose trade is in the dollar?

The integration and acceptance of advanced functionality and the adoption of Bitcoin within the institutional space, especially for those traditionally involved in dollar-denominated investments, can be daunting. Overcoming the psychological discomfort experienced when individuals hold conflicting beliefs can be daunting.

As the Bitcoin market matures, it is becoming more institutionally friendly. This means institutions are warming to Bitcoin, not the other way around. The development of robust infrastructure, including secure custodial solutions, derivatives markets, and regulated exchanges, has increased institutional investors' attraction to Bitcoin. This is a flawed attraction, but an attraction, nonetheless.

The coming ETF has shown tacit approval. The development of financial instruments, such as Bitcoin futures and other derivatives, allows institutions to gain exposure to Bitcoin without directly holding the underlying asset. This financialization process provides additional tools for risk management and fits within the traditional investment framework. There are drawbacks to allowing intuitional intrusion. I should have started with this vital acronym and warning NYKNYC—not your keys, not your coins.

The emergence of secure and institutional-grade custody solutions has addressed concerns about the safe storage of digital assets. Institutions can now rely on specialized custodians to securely hold and manage their Bitcoin holdings. NYKNYC!

Acceptance of Digital Assets

As the broader financial industry starts to recognize the legitimacy of digital assets, institutions are more willing to explore and invest in this Bitcoin asset class. You can now be the first kid on your block. Positive narratives around Bitcoin's potential as a store of value and answer to the inflation problem have contributed to its acceptance.

The entry of traditional financial players, such as major banks, asset management firms, and hedge funds, into the Bitcoin space has signaled a shift in perception. These players bring institutional expertise, regulatory relationships, and a level of credibility that can influence institutions steeped in the dollar to overcome cognitive dissonance. I enjoy watching this fear and greed relationship play out.

The economic landscape, including low interest rates, concerns about fiat currency devaluation, and the search for alternative investments, has prompted institutions to diversify their portfolios. Bitcoin, is in exceptionally limited supply and non-correlated to all other investments in this context.

Bitcoin's positive price performance and the fear of missing out (FOMO) on potential gains have seeped into institutional decision-making. As Bitcoin has demonstrated resilience and attracted attention, institutions may feel compelled to participate to avoid missing out on a growing market.

The Unbanked Benefits

The term, "unbanked" refers to individuals who do not have access to traditional banking services. Approximately 40% of the global population cannot find financial inclusion. In short, these individuals need a bank account, making it challenging for them to participate in formal economic systems. Bitcoin offers financial inclusion to the unbanked, providing them with a self-directed means of accessing and managing their finances. People in developing countries need more access to traditional banking services due to inadequate infrastructure or geographic constraints. Bitcoin can provide a decentralized and accessible financial system for these populations, allowing them to send and receive funds without the need for a traditional bank account.

Bitcoin can also facilitate cross-border transactions, enabling migrant workers to send remittances to their families more efficiently and with less friction than traditional remittance services.

Refugees and displaced populations often face difficulties in establishing financial identities. Young individuals and students who have not yet established a formal banking relationship may find Bitcoin more accessible.

Many individuals around the world work in the informal economy, where traditional banking services may be difficult to access. Bitcoin provides an alternative for these workers to engage in financial transactions since it is now their money without relying on traditional banking infrastructure.

Some people may be excluded from traditional banking services due to a poor credit history. Because Bitcoin is a digital bearer asset, Bitcoin transactions are not dependent on credit scores or KYC (know your customer rules). You don't even need a driver's license.

It might be worth noting here that never before in history has there been anything like this bearer asset. Bitcoin is often referred to as a "bearer asset" due to the nature of its ownership and transferability. A bearer asset is an asset that is legally owned by whoever holds it, and ownership is not registered with any central authority. With Bitcoin, ownership is determined by control over the private key associated with a Bitcoin wallet. If you possess the private key, you have control over the associated Bitcoins.

While Bitcoin transactions are recorded on a public ledger, users' identities are not directly tied to their wallet addresses. This provides a degree of pseudonymity and privacy, reinforcing the bearer asset characteristic. The focus is on controlling the private key rather than revealing personal information.

Conferences and Meetups

$$$ Bitcoiners and venture capitalists often interact at various events, conferences, and meetups within the Bitcoin space. These gatherings provide a platform for individuals interested in Bitcoin and blockchain technology at Bitcoin conferences or meetups.

There is a well-known Bitcoin conference taking place today in many major cities; these conferences attract a diverse audience of Bitcoin enthusiasts, developers, entrepreneurs, and investors. Venture capitalists interested in Bitcoin, decentralized technologies, and blockchain projects may attend such events to explore investment opportunities. The conference includes networking sessions, where attendees can mingle, exchange ideas, and build connections. Bitcoiners, including developers, early adopters, industry professionals, and perhaps yourself, use these opportunities to share experiences and insights.

The conference may host panels or discussions featuring venture capitalists. These sessions provide insights into investment trends, strategies, and the types of projects venture capitalists are interested in supporting. This is happening every day in every major city in the world. By participating in these events, Bitcoiners and venture capitalists engage in meaningful conversations, share perspectives, and explore potential collaborations. Friends are made quickly because the Bitcoin culture fosters comradery the deeper you venture down the rabbit hole. These interactions play a crucial role in fostering innovation, supporting the growth of the Bitcoin ecosystem, and facilitating investment in promising projects within the space.

Internet to Bitcoin Comparison

The evolution of Bitcoin can be compared to the evolution of the Internet in several ways, as both represent transformative technologies that have changed the way we interact, transact, and communicate. There are some parallels between the evolution of the Internet and the evolution of Bitcoin. Bitcoin is a powerful communication tool for freedom of speech; hence, the censorship resistance feature allows you to voice your opinion with your wallet. Talk may be cheap, but not when it is said with

Bitcoin. And this as the Internet is losing its censorship resistant luster.

Early innovation and enthusiast adoption paved the way for the Internet, primarily used by researchers and enthusiasts. The development of the World Wide Web and the creation of the first web browsers brought the Internet to a broader audience. Prodigy was my first foray into the Internet, which was then a glorified bulletin board.

In its early days, Bitcoin was embraced by a niche community of cryptography enthusiasts and individuals interested in decentralized systems. **Satoshi Nakamoto's** release of the Bitcoin whitepaper in 2008 marked the beginning of its development.

The Internet is built on a set of protocols and technologies, including TCP/IP, HTTP, and HTML. These foundational technologies enabled the creation of websites, online communication, and e-commerce, which we enjoy every day.

Bitcoin is built on blockchain technology and cryptographic principles. The blockchain serves as a decentralized and immutable ledger, enabling secure and transparent peer-to-peer transactions, without the need for intermediaries. It is soon to be enjoyed every day by everyone, everywhere.

The Internet, in its early days, faced skepticism and misconceptions. Some questioned its practical applications, and there were concerns about security and privacy.

Bitcoin has faced similar skepticism, with early concerns about its legitimacy, security, and use cases. As with the Internet, increased understanding and adoption have helped address these concerns. Bitcoin has a significant advantage: It is layered atop the already accomplished infrastructure of the Internet, which took quite a bit of time to develop. Bitcoin is on a greased glide path to adoption.

The Internet gradually transitioned from a niche technology to an essential part of daily life. As more people gained access to the Internet, new use cases emerged, including email, search engines, and social media.

Bitcoin has experienced a similar but speedier trajectory, with growing awareness and adoption over time. While still in the process of mainstream adoption, Bitcoin has gained recognition as a form of digital gold and an answer to inflation.

The Internet's ecosystem expanded with the development of diverse applications, including e-commerce, social networking, streaming services, and cloud computing.

The Bitcoin ecosystem has grown to include various applications and services, such as exchanges, wallets, decentralized finance (DeFi) platforms, and more. Additionally, blockchain technology has been applied beyond Bitcoin in areas like supply chain management.

Ongoing innovation and technological advancements have continued to shape the Internet. The development of Web 2.0, mobile Internet, and the Internet of Things (IoT) are examples of subsequent iterations.

Bitcoin, too, continues to undergo development and innovation. Improvements in scalability (e.g., the Lightning Network), privacy features, and smart contract capabilities are among the areas where ongoing innovation occurs.

The Internet has profoundly impacted global communication, commerce, education, and entertainment, transforming industries and societies.

Bitcoin, while still relatively young compared to the Internet, will bring about significant changes in the financial landscape. It introduces a decentralized form of money and not only challenges traditional notions of currency and value transfer; it will be the dominant world medium of exchange, store of value, and unit of account.

In summary, both the Internet and Bitcoin represent revolutionary technologies that have transformed and continue to shape various aspects of our lives and integration into global systems. The overriding theme of this book is to bring awareness of the opportunity in Bitcoin now, versus later, when Bitcoin is ubiquitous; thereby allowing you, the reader, to avail yourself of the tremendous opportunity.

Bitcoin Regulation

Bitcoin is a dynamic technology, and its regulation is unable to keep pace with innovation.

The regulation of Bitcoin often faces challenges in keeping pace with the evolving nature of the blockchain and Bitcoin ecosystem.

Even though the Bitcoin protocol is simple in nature, Bitcoin's underlying technology, the blockchain is complex and constantly improving. The rapid development of new features and applications can outpace the ability of regulatory bodies to grasp and respond fully to these innovations. The built-in rules, such as consensus, are so strong that regulation isn't needed and only serves to muddy the waters. Bitcoin will be adopted with or without regulation.

Bitcoin operates independently on a global and decentralized network, whether regulation exists or not. This makes it challenging for individual countries or regulatory bodies striving to establish a uniform set of rules that aren't needed. The decentralized nature of Bitcoin transcends national borders, creating regulatory complexities. The square peg attempting to fit in a round hole so they can get their piece is superfluous.

The rapid growth of decentralized finance (DeFi) introduces new and innovative financial products and services built on blockchain technology. DeFi operates without traditional intermediaries, challenging existing regulatory frameworks we all have come to know and live with.

Due to the fast-paced and innovative nature of Bitcoin, there is a growing recognition among regulators of the need for flexible and adaptive regulatory frameworks. Some jurisdictions are exploring regulatory sandboxes and other approaches to foster innovation while ensuring consumer protection and market integrity. They will do what they do, and Bitcoin will do what it does best. The market is accepting Bitcoin despite regulatory frameworks. The regulators would like you to think they are dangling an ETF low-hanging fruit, but they eventually had to offer it as Bitcoin would move forward with or without, whatever they pretend to offer.

National Debt Interest

The interest on the US debt is approaching one or more trillion dollars this year and every subsequent year. I only say this to contrast Bitcoins market cap today, which is approaching one trillion dollars. If everyone sold all of their Bitcoin today to donate it all to the national debt, it would only be a drop in the bucket to paying off the interest only on our "reported" national debt. America's ginormous 33 trillion dollar debt mountain is only the tip of the iceberg. The actual national debt is well in excess of this number by an order of magnitude when calculating all liabilities, such as social security. I don't even know how those two words can be placed next to each other. Unknown opaque debt and free flowing corruption debt flow into "war zones." Bankrupt pensions leave those who trusted this system in slave dependency in an insecure social secureness for as long as it works or doesn't. Do not get me started.

Auditability

Don't just trust; "trust but verify" was Ronald Regan's mantra. Is the gold in the vault? Are there reserves in those banks? Maybe or maybe not! Today, who can say? Gold or dollars, there is only a sketchy, vague idea of how much exists or doesn't. Where is it at any particular time? With Bitcoin, verification is so easy a caveman can do it for free 24/7. Simply and confidently put the Bitcoin address in the search line at https://www.blockchain.com/explorer.

Clean books and corporate hygiene are highly desired, especially when a sale of your company is impending. All interested parties, including bondholders or shareholders, love this and open transparent snapshots of the business.

- Clean and accurate financials tell the honest story of any business. The balance sheet includes things owned (assets) and things owed (liabilities). Assets minus liabilities equals owners' equity.

- Financial statements are written records that convey the business activities and the financial performance of an entity.
- The balance sheet provides an overview of assets, liabilities, and shareholders' equity as a snapshot in time.
- The income statement primarily focuses on a company's revenues and expenses.
- The cash flow statement (CFS) measures how well a company generates cash to pay its debt obligations.

This being said, corporate hygiene is generally neglected and even sometimes obfuscated, especially on government books.

Props to Bitwise, who will actually show you the reserve verification! Bitwise was the first to offer a proof of reserve model. Bitwise **Leads the Way in Bitcoin ETF Transparency.** The implications of this are enormous. With Bitcoin, all financial institutions can now show backing or even collateralize themselves if need be. All custodians can offer the same transparent audit. Before now, you couldn't secure a loan this easily, even with physical gold. And your Bitcoins don't need to be at risk, either. Proof of collateral is what will be required. All finance will gravitate to a transformative metamorphosis of this financial camouflage. Bitcoin has the ability to be 100% auditable. It is not just a snapshot like in traditional finance, but a dynamic live streaming, constantly audited issue if desired.

And the pressure will be on, as the public becomes aware of Bitcoin's deepest desire to be publicly transparent.

Imagine asking the Fort Knox vault to show us an immutable ledger of all verified content of their gold and where it is and to the millionth of a cent how much there is. This audit could be viewable by everyone, all of the time, in real-time. We all know this magical audit is laughable. But with Bitcoin, you can put an alert on your phone when an ounce moves one inch. So Sorry, not only isn't this possible with gold, but I wonder if many of us would want to look for the dread of our gut knowledge. A candid audit would only prove our worst fear.

Bitcoin can accomplish the task for all financialized assets. Not only can it, but it was built to do that very thing. Bitcoin adoption is unfolding rather than being revealed in an instant because we are afraid of seeing just what the man behind the curtain is up to. We are comfortable with our normalcy bias, soaking in a nice warm bath of frog soup. Make no mistake; Bitcoin adoption will unfold.

Deflationary World

Because we all grew up in an inflationary world, we never realized that the natural world around us always gravitates to deflation.

It actually has been ingrained into us that deflation is the biggest boogieman to fight. Frankly, deflation is a cute puppy and our friend. We try our best to accomplish deflation with each and every transaction made in our lives. When we buy trinkets or gasoline or anything of value, we ask that the purveyors of these things keep prices low and, if at all possible, free. Air and water are free sometimes. They are precious at certain other times, such as when they become scarce.

Living in an Inflationary and Deflationary World

Inflation and deflation are not exclusively separate. They coexist, one to our benefit and the other to our detriment, simultaneously without really anyone noticing. Sometimes, the prices of goods are inflationary, and sometimes, our wages are deflationary simultaneously, especially in contrast to each other. Years ago, my wife used to take pictures of our family with a Kodak color Polaroid. Snap, snap, a dollar, dollar, snap, dollar. I would cringe after 50 or so snaps. Later, I found a way to take pictures for free, lowering the marginal cost of production to zero. This is deflation. I know that this is dating me, but at the same time, the Polaroid picture of my new Corvette was less than $6000; the car, that is, not the picture. Today, I can't afford that new Corvette exceeding $100,000.00, or the Polaroid for that matter. Many items selectively get cheaper depending on predominantly, the marginal cost of production. This mixed with the system's desire to "encourage us" to modify behavior. For example, televisions are getting cheaper all the time.

This kind of thing is pervasive and controls our lives and collective desire to maintain a dollar system. The manipulators used to be three steps ahead, but because of Bitcoin, they are only one step ahead. Soon to be vanquished. Where will you stand when this happens? Pushing a wheelbarrow full of cash for kindling, or will you have converted it for something better?

Financial repression continues to shield the corrupt thieves and a bankrupt system. Bitcoin is indestructible. Oscar Wilde once astutely remarked, "Nowadays people know the **price of everything** and the **value of nothing."** This cynical observation from his novel "<u>THE PICTURE OF DORIAN GRAY</u>" highlights the tendency of modern society to focus on material worth, while overlooking more profound, intrinsic value.

Wilde's words serve as a timeless reminder to consider not only the monetary cost but also the true significance and worth of things. Perhaps, in a world obsessed with transactions, we should pause to appreciate the intangible riches that surround us such as autonomy, privacy and freedom.

VIOLENT UPSIDE

This is the down-and-dirty meat and potatoes of this book. Sure, some on the Internet hyperbolically say watch for the moonshot to a million dollars. I am saying the same exact thing but with reasoning and a clear path to reach 10 million and much higher. Strap in! Elevated prices will cause bank runs and bids coming out of the woodwork, and no supply will be found with a searchlight.

Markets are fundamentally driven by forces of the law of supply and demand.

Supply is the quantity of a good or service that producers are willing and able to sell into the market.

Demand, on the other hand, represents the quantity of a good or service that consumers are willing and able to buy at various price levels.

Equilibrium is the point where the supply and demand curves intersect. At this point, the quantity supplied equals the quantity demanded, and the market is said to be in equilibrium. The interaction of supply and demand determines the equilibrium price and quantity.

If there is a shortage e.g. demand exceeds supply at the current price, prices tend to rise, encouraging producers to supply more; but in the case of Bitcoin there is a fixed and diminishing supply. Keep this salient point handy in your mind.

My thesis, which will play out repeatedly on ad infinitum, leads us to focus on the equilibrium price. I see this as eventually getting to a point where Bitcoin price **only** goes up in price and will do so in ever more giant and larger leaps until demand is eventually satisfied. This will engulf the entire world's wealth through complete adoption. And it will not even stop there, as production efficiencies ramp up as the need for taxes is reduced; this as a result of reduced state corruption and the big one is an elimination of inflation. The immutability and transparency of Bitcoin will expose and prevent the political and elitist classes from acting with impunity against the public interest. Bitcoin keeps an immutable ledger, holding those accountable for corruption running for the hills—those elitists used to attempt to create war as cover, but no more. Bitcoin will hold them accountable because the ledger is immutable. The natural state of the economy being deflationary and the unnatural state of the economy being inflationary will begin to correct for corruption and create a better world. Quit voting for liars, both Democrat and Republican. Vote against the lying dollar. Make some meaningful votes. Vote to free Julian Assange and Edward Snowden. Start to arrange your life to free yourself by hoarding Bitcoin and shedding and spending dollars not just because it will make you rich but also because it will make you free.

Pseudonymity: Bitcoin transactions are pseudonymous. While wallet addresses are public, they do not directly reveal the user's identity. This provides a level of privacy compared to traditional financial systems, where personal information is often tied to transactions.

Censorship Resistance: Bitcoin operates on a decentralized blockchain. A network of miners verifies transactions, and no central authority can arbitrarily censor or block transactions. This is especially relevant in countries with restrictive financial regulations or political censorship.

Permissionless: Anyone can participate in the Bitcoin network without needing approval from a central authority. You don't need permission to create a wallet for free, I might add, to send or receive funds or participate in mining.

Immutable Transactions: Once a transaction is confirmed on the Bitcoin blockchain, it becomes part of an immutable ledger. No one can alter or reverse it. This feature ensures that your financial history remains intact and impervious to tampering.

Self-Custody: With Bitcoin, you have complete control over your private keys. You can store your funds securely in a wallet without relying on banks or third parties. This self-custody virtually eliminates the risk of asset seizure or freezing.

Global Accessibility: Bitcoin transcends borders without intermediaries.

Bitcoin Sooner than Later

Market dynamics in Bitcoin's early years are affected by changes in factors such as consumer preferences, production costs, external events, and government policies, leading to changes in market prices. These market dynamics will fade over time compared to Bitcoin's supply and demand dynamics. Normalcy bias related to traditional investing will be replaced with exponential growth as the market moves from its love affair with traditional finance and races toward a new reserve asset, Bitcoin. Hypersupply demand imbalances will become the norm. People and institutions will begin to trip over each other as if there were a fire in the theater, panicking for an exit from dollars. People will start to realize how ridiculous it was not to try and understand and appreciate Bitcoin a bit earlier—500 million and then one billion, then two, three billion per day ETF demand. Right now, the natural supply from mining is 900 Bitcoins per day. The ETF alone will swamp that now. In the April halving, only 450 Bitcoin will be produced. That's 10x-20x-30x or more of the natural supply. I'm not including retail demand. I'm not including institutional demand. I'm not including the 4 billion unbanked market. I'm not including sovereign demand. As good of an investment as Google, Apple, and Microsoft have been, all of these pee wees together could not come close to absorbing 100 trillion dollars. Bitcoin could, though, and a hundred times more with ease. We are at the top of the first inning between the Peewees and the NY Yankees. Get in now or get in never.

Complete ownership and control is when you hold Bitcoin. You have direct ownership and control over your funds. No intermediaries can freeze your account or impose restrictions. Once you obtain an address (Bitcoin wallet), simply cut and paste your address to fund your account. No fear of anyone looking over your shoulder because there is NO NEED to reveal or mess with your private key, which is securely locked away in your vault.

Supply Shock

At this point, understanding the dynamics of Bitcoin supply and demand will become more important and crucial for analyzing market behavior and prices as we proceed. The supply/demand function appears to be able to find an equilibrium currently. This will not necessarily hold true in the near future. For now, this is the market price of Bitcoin. But hang on to your hats!

What if the natural supply shrank or even disappeared? Put on your thinking cap for a moment. Bitcoin is constantly reducing its supply right now with the halving. Eventually, Bitcoin will be exhausted of any natural supply at all, unlike gold, which is still in the ground, albeit in lower ore quality.

This supply shock will be compounded by destroyed and lost Private keys to Bitcoin. These lost Bitcoin enriches the whole ecosphere fairly and will raise the price as those lucky enough to own Bitcoin understand this value boost. Imagine if a water boy carried something valuable, such as a canteen of drinking water, on a trek through the desert. The temperatures with the sun beating down topped 115 degrees. You are blissfully unaware that the water boy has been drinking regularly and, worse yet, accidentally spilled half of the water. Do you think the balance of the water is more or less valuable? What if a group accompanied you on your hike through the desert? More valuable? What if everyone in the world were on this desert adventure? My point is that Bitcoin supply shock is a reality today and is going to get much worse; not just zero supply, but negative supply as keys are lost and only HODLers arrive and drive todays 71% HODLers to 98% HODLers and beyond. This realization will overwhelms the masses; custodians will HODL, governments will HODL, and I will HODL, guaranteed.

Demand Shock

Currently, there is a demand shock if you look through the 14-year history of Bitcoin's life. The average percent increase has been unmatched by any other asset, stock, tulip, or any other mania conceived of from the beginning of time. But there is nothing like the demand shock to come. Bitcoin at $40,000 per Bitcoin is 99.9% off its future price. Currently, there exists a market equilibrium. Who can say? Will offers slow or stop? I will tell you here, and now that demand will grow and grow. RIA will require investors to take 1%, then 2%, then 5%, and the requirement when the monthly statements arrive in investors' hands becomes a demand for a higher allocation—15%, 25% for some lucky ones, all in. Remember the dodo bird, a flightless bird native to Mauritius in the Indian Ocean. European explorers arrived in the 1600s, and Dutch sailors unfortunately ate these large, heavy birds to extinction.

When the Fire Starts

When the fire starts, market equilibrium will vanish as the price literally will not find an offer. Let me elucidate. Beginning with the Bitcoin spot ETF buyers, which may increase by a factor of 900% or more. Buyers will wake up to a continuous news cycle that shows Bitcoin rising each day for weeks and months on end due to ETF buyers. ETF investors don't even need to request Bitcoin investment; typically, their investment contract instructs the RIA's to place specific allocations of any new asset class into their portfolio. This will lead to boundless FOMO. Even though I don't recommend purchasing the Bitcoin spot ETF, but only the underlying asset, nevertheless, Bitcoin's price will be forced up. This rise will lead to an eventual tipping point whereby all assets will rush for the exit and then through an ever-shrinking Bitcoin door, an entrance the size of the eye of a needle. First, possibly anything fiat-related: pesos, yen, dollars, then bonds and stocks in a moment of clarity for those markets. Then it may come in waves, because they are not as liquid, real-estate, gold, artwork or anything of value will wash into Bitcoin. Why? Because Bitcoin works like nothing else. Bitcoin is the difference between a dying monetary system and the hardest money in the world.

People are just starting to question property rights. Bank bail-ins and reach-ins to take money from your account used to be unthinkable; these are now carried out worldwide by governments and related agencies like FinCen, the Department of Homeland Security, the IRS, and so on. Bitcoin, being utterly resistant to confiscation or seizure, is wholly isolated from the powers that be.

Consider where we stand right now. Bitcoin is treated as a pariah, a leper, and even an outlaw compared to what it will be: a heroic, honest, durable, hardest money in the world. Institutions are sitting up and taking notice. This may be the best price to buy this value proposition ever. Most people understand Bitcoin not, and even fewer people own any. Bitcoin imposes a discipline of engineered truth in money. Bitcoin is the most vital, most reliable money on planet Earth, and being accepted by financial institutions right now. Who is going to want moth-eaten dollars or what they can't buy one or five years down the road? What a miraculous time to learn the Bitcoin value proposition.

My quick advice is to stop reading this book and convert ten percent of your assets into Bitcoin; even if you don't understand it, you can buy the ETF temporarily and convert it to actual Bitcoin as soon as you learn how to place it securely into a paper wallet. Later in this book, I will provide directions and access to how to get and fund your secure paper wallet.

Consider that the dollar wanes because countries other than the USA don't like the control that comes with the dollar. Oil, which is typically priced in dollars worldwide, may be taken up by the natural dollar replacement. Some large sovereigns have already shunned the muscle flexing of the USA and unilaterally trade for oil in their own currency, flirting with war.

Random Thoughts Lightning Round

Because I am anxious to put this book in the hands of readers so that they can benefit, I will publish my notes in a slightly less organized way over the following few pages. The dollar, the best fiat currency, degrades @ 7.5% annually. Thus, Bitcoin, without adding new adoption or any other changes, makes 7.5% by default in comparison and is on top of the best fiat in the world.

Candidates for President are coming out for Bitcoin.

Bitcoin is young and early, but it is not an untested issue.

The Internet changed the way people communicate. Bitcoin changes the way people communicate wealth.

The first published rate of 1309 Bitcoins equaled one dollar, in October of 2009, about 13 Bitcoins for a penny. Today, this represents a 5 billion percent increase.

The white paper is posted at the end of this book. It provided a road map to open-source software; anyone can look at it.

Censorship resistance: Julian Assange donations were blocked by Visa, PayPal, and MasterCard, not Bitcoin, though! That is "freedom of speech."

Digital currency is already happening in dollars.

If you convert dollars to Bitcoin, it is still a worthy digital currency without theft, lies, inflation, tax, drug wars, pyramid schemes... I wonder why a spying pyramid is on the reverse of a dollar bill. Hmmmm?

Bitcoin players and venture capitalists are meeting right now!

Bitpay converts Bitcoin to dollars and eliminates volatility of Bitcoin if you prefer; and carries less than a third of the commission associated with credit cards instantly. Why process with credit cards? Why even use dollar-denominated credit cards, for that matter?

Credit cards should be a gigantic antitrust lawsuit in the making. Because everything we do or buy costs us three percent more than someone using Bitcoin or even cash, for that matter, that's not fair to cash users. I wonder why regulators are selective in their persecutions.

Bitcoin has yet to become mainstream, leaving lots of room for price growth. Bitcoin is the only logical way forward.

It is counter-intuitive that wealthy Americans have no need for Bitcoin, but the unbanked third world does.

Regulation cannot keep pace with innovation and technology. Let's let it live and do its own thing without the system front-running every innovation.

BlackRock's proposed spot Bitcoin ETF received the ticker symbol IBIT according to an amended S-1 filing with the SEC. They bite.

An early Biblical surveillance census was done during the birth of Christ. Some things just never change.

Bitcoin maturity has different meanings, i.e., when Bitcoin was brand new in 2009, the dollar conversion was 1300 Bitcoins to a dollar, and no one conceived of Bitcoin as replacing the dollar. Today, Bitcoin is $43,000 per Bitcoin, and very few conceive of Bitcoin replacing the dollar in the near future. Someday soon, everyone will understand that dollars are going the way of the horse and buggy, and one Satoshi will equate to 1 cent.

Fed cuts make people happy. But the Fed is there to steal your opportunity and, money and blessings. They will reign in Bitcoin purchases in an attempt at a controlled assent and create volatility to shake you out.

The drawback with Bitcoin spot ETF purchase is that it's not your keys and not your coin.

$$$ FVA – Fair Value Accounting Transition

$$$ Digital assets are minimally allocated so far. Real estate, gold, stocks, and bonds will move into Bitcoin to remove risk and increase yield.

$$$ ETF optimism will drag Bitcoin into a new level of maturity. Warning – if you are new to Bitcoin and buy into the ETF, be sure to learn at least how to self-custody. Remove the real risk and replace the ETF with ownership of Bitcoin via (self-custody).

$$$ A crisis of confidence in the dollar.

This just in.... Passage of an emergency spending bill in support of a supercharged FED printing press, containing a turbocharger to help with continued debt ceiling elevation mechanisms; film at 11.

$$$ The next milestone is that a central bank holds Bitcoin. Fact, then five central banks, then ten....

Explain FTX facts vs the pattern of indicting SBF via the threat of pointing fingers in exchange for safety—all this to slow the Bitcoin ETF rollout; so the big banks can get *their piece.* This is in light of actual swollen demand.

Savings audit – immutability is confirmed on Bitcoin layer one. Spending – is better on layer two.

People of note: Lyn Alden, Andreas Antonopoulos, Michael Saylor.

Dollar addictions will wane, and the psychological barrier will drop.

BlackRock acts like blowfish or greater sage grouse to scare the market into submission to keep markets low till they can capitalize.

$$$ Fair value accounting FASB has been approved.

$$$ Banks are beginning to custody Bitcoin and lending against it.

$$$ Fully decentralized network is entirely secure.

Do the opposite, of what the tapeworms say that they do. – Jamie Diamond, Elizabeth Warren, Gary Gensler.

Bitcoin is under an incessant and constant unsuccessful attack—fourteen years of repelled attacks.

$$$ Bitcoin will migrate to encompass a 700 trillion dollar worldwide market.

Bitcoin is a legitimate asset. Bitcoin works, is hack proof, and will be believed to be the world's hardest money or reserve asset.

The killer app is being worked on right now as I wait for Bitcoin to go to a $1 million equivalency.

Securely spend and transfer from secure cold storage.

The Lightning Network is working now and increased twenty thousand percent last year.

A confluence of demand and supply shock, the halving as a catalyst for supply reduction, and the ETF demand will lead to sticker shock.

Shake off worthless news, such as an unnamed analyst suggesting a price correction with no facts, will pop up like "whack a mole." Don't even bother reading them; certainly don't react. Get a position and HODL.

Alt (shitcoins) diversion akin to an infertile mosquito release. Crypto vs. Bitcoin.

Ignore the noise and news. Bitcoin will plow through it.

Congratulations to the new owners of Bitcoin.

Being anti-Bitcoin is bad political policy, and those like Elizabeth Warren will be gone soon.

We may be dragged into the future of digital money.

$$$ More fiat will be forced into Bitcoin this year than all of Bitcoin history.

While big banks were late to the game, they will make it up as big stack poker players, manipulating the market. Use your HODL technique.

Those who are on the outside of Bitcoin will suffer.

Predominantly well-banked and the relatively comfortable, will have the most normalcy bias and shun Bitcoin for a while until it cannot further be denied: "Everyone gets Bitcoin at the price that they deserve."

Staying wrong is a sin, and your sins will manifest themselves. Bitcoin is not going away, and we all get Bitcoin at the price we deserve.

$$$ Laser eyes makes harder money.

In viewing the last three cycles, a Christmas tree appears. Markets will not be held to some normalcy bias – 100X is possible during this next cycle. 1000x over the next cycle after this. We are not in a fiat dollar world. We are in Bitcoin world. Please do not believe me; check for yourself or sit on the sidelines with your schwanz in your hand.

$$$ BlackRock and manipulator banks are not a force for good.

But, because they are forced to advance it, the Bitcoin market will get a prodigious burst of appreciation for at least four or five years and free marketing jingle bells all the way.

$$$ Manipulator banks think they have a plan to corral it and propagandize it down. Then, they will buy as much of it as they possibly can.

$$$ Global Bitcoin sovereign adoption. Argentina's Bitcoin adoption.

$$$ Javier Milei won the presidency in Argentina. He is an austerity president and ran on a Bitcoin platform.

$$$ El Salvador and Argentina seem to be leaning toward the dollar, and this may be a stepping stone to Bitcoin becoming a reserve asset.

$$$ Bitcoin is the most important technological advancement in a thousand years!

Bitcoin is Energy

The base layer of all wealth is energy. Take just a second to think this out: Every item requires oil to produce, transport, and run. This includes cars, houses, plastic in pens, all appliances, computers, and Bitcoin miners—literally everything.

The annual value of oil traded worldwide can vary depending on factors such as oil prices, production levels, and global demand. Global oil trade for the entire year could be in the hundreds of millions of barrels annually. If oil were financed in Bitcoin instead of dollars, this could amount to twenty-six million Bitcoins at today's price by itself every year. There aren't even that many Bitcoins. The friction of the oil trade when traded in Bitcoin would be cut by 99.7% and completely verifiable instantly.

Because of Bitcoin's transparency, large sums of money can be tracked, and the likelihood of wars and terrorism would be diminished or eliminated. Perhaps, as a result, production would increase, and natural deflation would make for a better world.

Exchange Order Book

An exchange order book is a real-time, continuously updated list of buy and sell orders on a trading platform for a particular financial instrument, such as a Bitcoin or a stock. The order book affords precise data about the current market demand and supply, allowing traders to follow price movements and make trading decisions.

Here's how an exchange order book works in this manner. The left side of the order book displays a list of buy orders or bids. These represent the prices at which traders are willing to purchase the financial instrument.

Each entry on the buy side includes the price and the corresponding quantity traders are looking to buy at that particular price or less.

The right side of the order book shows a list of sell orders or asks. These represent the prices traders are willing to sell in the same manor.

The order book is organized by price levels, with the highest bid and the lowest ask typically displayed at the top. The prices are usually arranged in descending order on the buy side and ascending order on the sell side.

Market depth refers to the cumulative quantity of buy and sell orders at different price levels. Traders often use market depth to assess the strength of the current market and identify potential support and resistance levels.

The difference between the highest bid and the lowest ask is known as the spread. A smaller spread is generally an indication of a more liquid market.

When a buy order matches a sell order at a specific price, a trade is executed. The order book is updated in real-time to reflect the new market conditions.

The order book is dynamic and can change rapidly as new orders are placed, existing orders are canceled, or trades are executed. Traders monitor these changes to adapt their strategies.

Bitcoin will eventually give this order book new meaning as Bitcoin adheres to no man's rule. What would an order book look like if there were no offers? Offers are thinning now, which is why we have a $40,000 Bitcoin price. But what if only a few people were left willing to part with their Bitcoin at any price? What if you were one of the few biddings on that half-full water canteen? What would the price be for a sip of water in an arid broiling desert?

A no-offer order book would necessitate a god candle that would ascend until some HODLer capitulated. If that were a sole HODLer, the price would be absorbed and continue to escalate higher. What if only a few owners of limited and scarce Bitcoin even allowed themselves to consider placing a very high offer, picking a number out of the air? A million, ten million? There would have to be opposing and then matching offers to bids. I would suggest that in the near future there will be many, many, more bids to buy than offers to sell. This requires little imagination.

Bitcoin is a new type of asset class in which assets will flow until there are no more assets. These assets are seeking a home or at least a safe harbor, perhaps gold, if it were easier to authenticate. Your attorney might bring a briefcase full of gold to a home closing, with witnesses and videos, to produce a receipt in acceptance of the home for gold trade.

Bitcoin can purchase a home with one click on your phone. The purchase will be documented remotely on the chain, an immutable ledger. No receipt is needed, and documentation no longer needs to be filed at the courthouse just to prove ownership.

I submit that stocks are linear and will follow a stock-to-flow model, with an ask for every bid. In a conventional box, what will it take to purchase your shares?

Bitcoin is currently following those linear attributes because people perceive Bitcoin as a stock-to-flow issue. The asks will slow at first, then there will be volatility, and then there will be no offers to sell except at an unimaginable price. Bitcoin will take on the attribute of "exponential only." It will be A Bitcoin musical chairs with all the chairs removed, except for the HODLers.

Do not worry you can reread this chapter for fun and with a telescopic look into the future. How do I know these things to be true? Because Bitcoin clearly provides superior property rights. Isn't that what you want? And your neighbors? I could be wrong.

You and your neighbors may prefer corruption in money and inflation and increasing income tax. I will agree that there remain a few statists and butt kissers, but most of us, as a consensus, will demand this new money, Not with picket signs but by moving your assets to Bitcoin gradually at first and then without notice. And let's be honest here; greed is a good motivator. Many will do it for freedom. Some because they have an Austrian school of economics affliction. RIAs registered Investment Advisors will put higher and higher allocations into Bitcoin. 401Ks will burst at the seams. Parabolic runs will ensue.

The Issuance of CBDCs

Banks are having to deal with both manufactured and real crises that they can't control. Banking crises are manufactured to corral and control the masses. Plans are constantly being devised, such as the issuance of CBDCs Central Bank Digital Currencies. These CBDCs carry spyware and other draconian elements. But guess what? The dollar is a CBDC. For the most part, dollars don't come off the printing press anymore. Dollars are printed digitally, which has been a surreptitious, sublime conversion. For the average citizen, the flow of dollar money is logged, surveilled, and issued SARs suspicious activity reports for lower and lower echelons of funds in and out of banks for the average citizen. These funds are examined and logged in such a way as to pinpoint what Joe Schmo is reading or wiping his behind with. The point is that dollars are already a CBDC. The threat of a new

CBDC is simply a diversion; a red herring hoisted up a flag pole to gauge a reaction. This ball of boogers and wax is what we should be comparing to Bitcoin. Bitcoin wins on every level. Central banks fear this and consider this comparison the nemesis crises that they need to fight and knowingly will eventually lose. This is the exact reason there is a Bitcoin ETF on the horizon; they are forming a "if you can't beat them, then join them" posture. It is "our faith," the consensus's faith, in which money wins. It is clear that Bitcoin, not monopoly money, will be the clear victor at the end of the day. What do you think will happen to the demand for Bitcoin when this all becomes clear and into focus?

Sovereigns

Nation states are replacing their favorite fiat and putting Bitcoin into its place. This is not theory; this is happening now. President Bukele is the President of El Salvador and a first mover to make Bitcoin a parallel currency with their own. President Bukele is a superstar in the South American region. Ready to be elected again with an 80% or better approval rating.   In other South American countries, campaign candidates paste selfies of Bukele and the candidate on campaign posters.

Many other nations are adopting Bitcoin and putting it on their balance sheets as the dominoes fall. What do you think will happen to the demand for Bitcoin when this becomes clear for these central bankers? And not just a fraction of the hardest money in the world, but all of their reserves converted to Bitcoin. These wheels are turning, and think tanks are considering the next move.

Obtain a Secure Paper Wallet

Air gapping a paper wallet is cumbersome and technically demanding.   I   will   direct   you to WWW.BITCOINMOUTH.COM, where you can obtain a secure air-gapped paper wallet.

An "air-gapped" paper Bitcoin wallet refers to a wallet that has been created and stored in a way that is entirely disconnected from the Internet or any network-connected device. This is done to enhance the security of the private key associated with the Bitcoin wallet. Exposure to online threats are eliminated.

Air-gapping omits the risk of online threats such as hacking, phishing, malware, and other cyberattacks that would otherwise compromise the security of a Bitcoin wallet. Keeping the wallet offline dispenses with the most vulnerable of attack surfaces. Of course, you must keep your Private Key of the key pair PRIVATE! Do not show it to anyone you do not intend.

An air-gapped paper wallet is not accessible remotely, making it immune to attacks that exploit vulnerabilities over the Internet. This protection is crucial as remote attacks are the primary vector for compromising online wallets. Since the wallet is kept offline, it cannot be used to initiate transactions without first being connected to a network. This adds an extra layer of security, as any transaction would require the wallet to be only temporarily connected to a device, reducing the risk of unauthorized access.

A paper wallet typically includes a private key and a corresponding public address. By keeping the wallet air-gapped, the private key is never exposed to online threats. Private keys are kept entirely offline. Air-gapped paper wallets are a form of cold storage, Cold storage is considered a completely secure way to store Bitcoin, as it is impenetrable to online vulnerabilities.

Creating an air-gapped paper wallet is a perfect solution for individuals who want to store Bitcoin for the long term and minimize the risk of online attacks. This is particularly relevant for those who prioritize security over frequent access to their funds. I recommend this as it is not particularly important right now to spend these funds or reconvert them back into worth less dollars. Only put a portion of your funds that you wish in the "real bank," a paper wallet for safekeeping. And let them grow as described earlier.

Transferring funds into or out of an air-gapped wallet will involve using a separate, HD hierarchical deterministic wallet for the transaction, which you can learn about later. At this initial juncture, if you don't already own Bitcoin, the preeminent action is for you to obtain a secure air-gapped wallet and fund it. Funding it is the easy part as you can provide the counterpart of your key pair (the address) to anyone at any time within reason. It is likened to the address of your home. You don't want everyone to have it, but you can openly provide it to a select few. This Bitcoin address is your funding address or (get paid) address. This is the simple essence of the Bitcoin wallet; it is the address and the private key combination or Key Pair. The private key is the very sensitive key to all the wealth you store in Bitcoin. This is likened to the key to your home. Do not give it to anyone except for whom you wish to enter and clean you out.

I personally only play with or test my various online or hardware wallets. Visit **https://testnet-faucet.com/**

It will take some time to become comfortable and trust these wallets. Honestly, it is irrelevant as I will not spend the hardest money I own. I will spend the fiat portion of my income or savings first to minimize exposure to inflation or, worse, confiscation or censorship of spending, corrupt seizures, and outright theft. I HODL.

Users should consider their security needs and the trade-offs involved in choosing different storage methods for their Bitcoin holdings. Additionally, proper backup procedures, as mentioned, should be followed to prevent the loss of funds in case of damage or loss of the paper wallet. This would include making copies and storing them in at least two separate locations, preferably with different secure areas at least two separate buildings apart from each other. The risk of fire or flood might require you to have an aluminum plate etched with your private key. Think carefully about your particular risk profile. These directions are a guide to making your easy-to-understand, most sensitive key or (password, if you will) trustworthy and completely private so you can sleep well.

This is a long-winded way to tell you about the simple essence of getting and funding a Bitcoin wallet. However, this is the exact reason ETFs were created to relieve you of this responsibility because this is precisely what the ETF purveyor and their custodians do. Then they charge you for this service, and you will have given up almost all the direct benefits of owning Bitcoin. You will only hold the shell of an index to Bitcoin. When you sell your ETF, you will receive funds back in dollars that may not be of **ANY VALUE!!** Fiat debasement is a 100% certainty. Bitcoin will rise by at least two orders of magnitude from here in the near future.

I hope this finds you better prepared to proceed with your Bitcoin endeavor. And happy parabolic runs!

1K3pm9a3gPEGPpKLAvzft53gbyUJnTY7tX

Use the QR code above or the Bitcoin address below it. If you wish to donate a few Sats to encourage me to write and go much deeper down the rabbit hole, with chapters such as how consensus money connects to faith or how and why to avoid fractionalized and ETF eggroll wrapped treasuries.

I will consolidate these donations and endow them to a truth cause and report back to you in my next book.

Send me your email address- for my personal files ONLY so I can provide you with a deep discount on my next book before it is published. And if you indicate, I will sign it for you.

Below I have supplied a copy of the original White Paper which is in the public domain:

Bitcoin: A Peer-to-Peer Electronic Cash System

Abstract

A purely peer-to-peer version of electronic cash would allow online payments to be sent directly from one party to another without going through a financial institution. Digital signatures provide part of the solution, but the main benefits are lost if a trusted third party is still required to prevent double-spending. We propose a solution to the double-spending problem using a peer-to-peer network. The network timestamps transactions by hashing them into an ongoing chain of hash-based proof-of-work, forming a record that cannot be changed without redoing the proof-of-work. The longest chain not only serves as proof of the sequence of events witnessed, but proof that it came from the largest pool of CPU power. As long as a majority of CPU power is controlled by nodes that are not cooperating to attack the network, they'll generate the longest chain and outpace attackers. The network itself requires minimal structure. Messages are broadcast on a best effort basis, and nodes can leave and rejoin the network at will, accepting the longest proof-of-work chain as proof of what happened while they were gone.

1. Introduction

Commerce on the Internet has come to rely almost exclusively on financial institutions serving as trusted third parties to process electronic payments. While the system works well enough for most transactions, it still suffers from the inherent weaknesses of the trust based model. Completely non-reversible transactions are not really possible, since financial institutions cannot avoid mediating disputes. The cost of mediation increases transaction costs, limiting the minimum practical transaction size and cutting off the possibility for small casual transactions, and there is a broader cost in the loss of ability to make non-reversible payments for non-reversible services. With the possibility of reversal, the need for trust spreads. Merchants must be wary of their customers, hassling them for more information than they would otherwise need. A certain percentage of fraud is accepted as unavoidable. These costs and payment uncertainties can be avoided in person by using physical currency, but no mechanism exists to make payments over a communications channel without a trusted party.

What is needed is an electronic payment system based on cryptographic proof instead of trust, allowing any two willing parties to transact directly with each other without the need for a trusted third party. Transactions that are computationally impractical to reverse would protect sellers from fraud, and routine escrow mechanisms could easily be implemented to protect buyers. In this paper, we propose a solution to the double-spending problem using a peer-to-peer distributed timestamp server to generate computational proof of the chronological order of transactions. The system is secure as long as honest nodes collectively control more CPU power than any cooperating group of attacker nodes.

2 . T r a n s a c t i o n s

We define an electronic coin as a chain of digital signatures. Each owner transfers the coin to the next by digitally signing a hash of the previous transaction and the public key of the next owner and adding these to the end of the coin. A payee can verify the signatures to verify the chain of ownership.

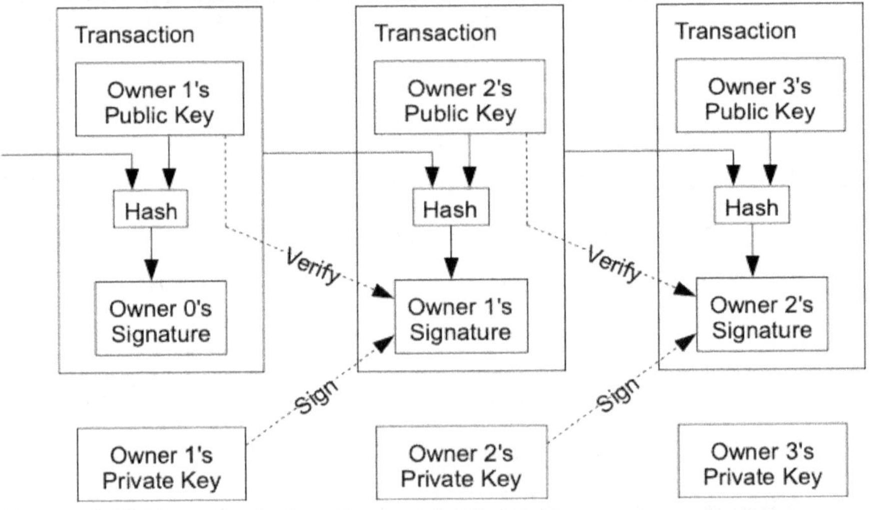

The problem of course is the payee can't verify that one of the owners did not double-spend the coin. A common solution is to introduce a trusted central authority, or mint, that checks every transaction for double spending. After each transaction, the coin must be returned to the mint to issue a new coin, and only coins issued directly from the mint are trusted not to be double-spent. The problem with this solution is that the fate of the entire money system depends on the company running the mint, with every transaction having to go through them, just like a bank.

We need a way for the payee to know that the previous owners did not sign any earlier transactions. For our purposes, the earliest transaction is the one that counts, so we don't care about later attempts to double-spend. The only way to confirm the absence of a transaction is to be aware of all transactions. In the mint based model, the mint was aware of all transactions and decided which arrived first. To accomplish this without a trusted party, transactions must be publicly announced[1], and we need a system for participants to agree on a single history of the order in which they were received. The payee needs proof that at the time of each transaction, the majority of nodes agreed it was the first received.

3. Timestamp Server

The solution we propose begins with a timestamp server. A timestamp server works by taking a hash of a block of items to be timestamped and widely publishing the hash, such as in a newspaper or Usenet post[2-5]. The timestamp proves that the data must have existed at the time, obviously, in order to get into the hash. Each timestamp includes the previous timestamp in its hash, forming a chain, with each additional timestamp reinforcing the ones before it.

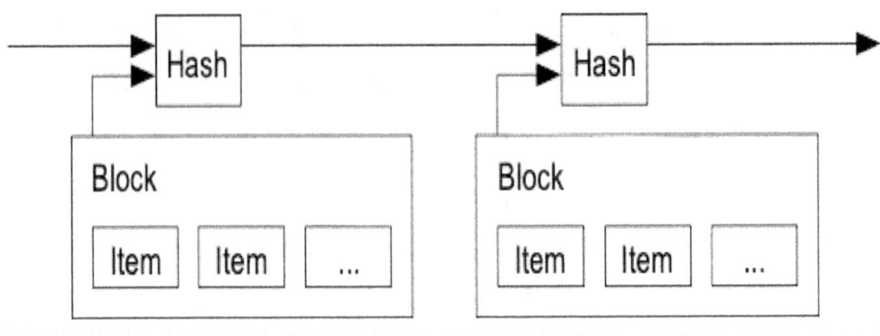

4. Proof-of-Work

To implement a distributed timestamp server on a peer-to-peer basis, we will need to use a proof-of-work system similar to Adam Back's Hashcash[6], rather than newspaper or Usenet posts. The proof-of-work involves scanning for a value that when hashed, such as with SHA-256, the hash begins with a number of zero bits. The average work required is exponential in the number of zero bits required and can be verified by executing a single hash.

For our timestamp network, we implement the proof-of-work by incrementing a nonce in the block until a value is found that gives the block's hash the required zero bits. Once the CPU effort has been expended to make it satisfy the proof-of-work, the block cannot be changed without redoing the work. As later blocks are chained after it, the work to change the block would include redoing all the blocks after it.

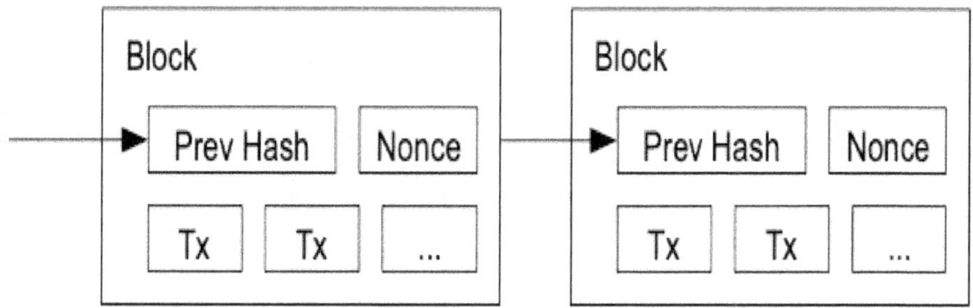

The proof-of-work also solves the problem of determining representation in majority decision making. If the majority were based on one-IP-address-one-vote, it could be subverted by anyone able to allocate many IPs. Proof-of-work is essentially one-CPU-one-vote. The majority decision is represented by the longest chain, which has the greatest proof-of-work effort invested in it. If a majority of CPU power is controlled by honest nodes, the honest chain will grow the fastest and outpace any competing chains. To modify a past block, an attacker would have to redo the proof-of-work of the block and all blocks after it and then catch up with and surpass the work of the honest nodes. We will show later that the probability of a slower attacker catching up diminishes exponentially as subsequent blocks are added.

To compensate for increasing hardware speed and varying interest in running nodes over time, the proof-of-work difficulty is determined by a moving average targeting an average number of blocks per hour. If they're generated too fast, the difficulty increases.

5. Network

The steps to run the network are as follows:

1. New transactions are broadcast to all nodes.
2. Each node collects new transactions into a block.
    3.Each node works on finding a difficult proof-of-work for its block.
3. When a node finds a proof-of-work, it broadcasts the block to all nodes.
4. Nodes accept the block only if all transactions in it are valid and not already spent.
5. Nodes express their acceptance of the block by working on creating the next block in the chain, using the hash of the accepted block as the previous hash.

Nodes always consider the longest chain to be the correct one and will keep working on extending it. If two nodes broadcast different versions of the next block simultaneously, some nodes may receive one or the other first. In that case, they work on the first one they received, but save the other branch in case it becomes longer. The tie will be broken when the next proof-of-work is found and one branch becomes longer; the nodes that were working on the other branch will then switch to the longer one.

New transaction broadcasts do not necessarily need to reach all nodes. As long as they reach many nodes, they will get into a block before long. Block broadcasts are also tolerant of dropped messages. If a node does not receive a block, it will request it when it receives the next block and realizes it missed one.

6. Incentive

By convention, the first transaction in a block is a special transaction that starts a new coin owned by the creator of the block. This adds an incentive for nodes to support the network, and provides a way to initially distribute coins into circulation, since there is no central authority to issue them. The steady addition of a constant of amount of new coins is analogous to gold miners expending resources to add gold to circulation. In our case, it is CPU time and electricity that is expended.

The incentive can also be funded with transaction fees. If the output value of a transaction is less than its input value, the difference is a transaction fee that is added to the incentive value of the block containing the transaction. Once a predetermined number of coins have entered circulation, the incentive can transition entirely to transaction fees and be completely inflation free.

The incentive may help encourage nodes to stay honest. If a greedy attacker is able to assemble more CPU power than all the honest nodes, he would have to choose between using it to defraud people by stealing back his payments, or using it to generate new coins. He ought to find it more profitable to play by the rules, such rules that favour him with more new coins than everyone else combined, than to undermine the system and the validity of his own wealth.

7. Reclaiming Disk Space

Once the latest transaction in a coin is buried under enough blocks, the spent transactions before it can be discarded to save disk space. To facilitate this without breaking the block's hash, transactions are hashed in a Merkle Tree [7][2][5], with only the root included in the block's hash. Old blocks can then be compacted by stubbing off branches of the tree. The interior hashes do not need to be stored.

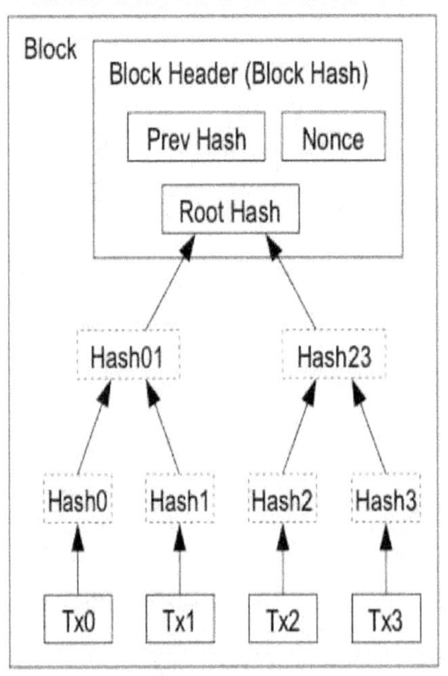

Transactions Hashed in a Merkle Tree

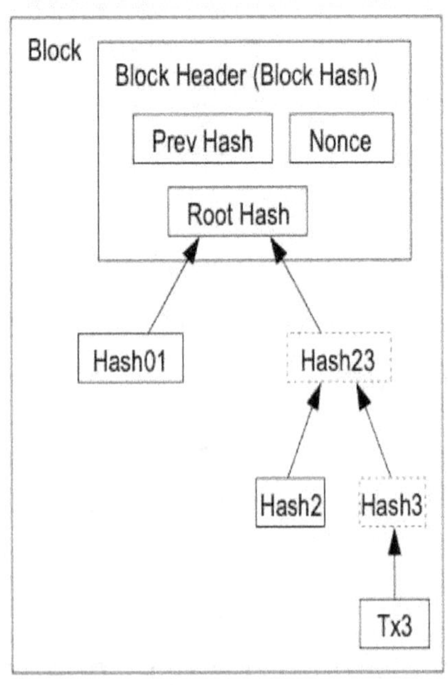

After Pruning Tx0-2 from the Block

A block header with no transactions would be about 80 bytes. If we suppose blocks are generated every 10 minutes, 80 bytes * 6 * 24 * 365 = 4.2MB per year. With computer systems typically selling with 2GB of RAM as of 2008, and Moore's Law predicting current growth of 1.2GB per year, storage should not be a problem even if the block headers must be kept in memory.

8. Simplified Payment Verification

It is possible to verify payments without running a full network node. A user only needs to keep a copy of the block headers of the longest proof-of-work chain, which he can get by querying network nodes until he's convinced he has the longest chain, and obtain the Merkle branch linking the transaction to the block it's timestamped in. He can't check the transaction for himself, but by linking it to a place in the chain, he can see that a network node has accepted it, and blocks added after it further confirm the network has accepted it.

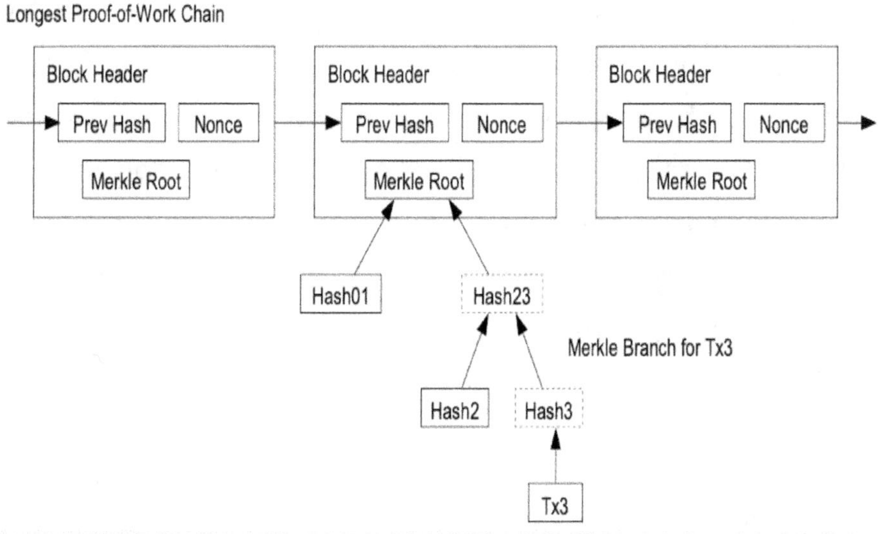

As such, the verification is reliable as long as honest nodes control the network, but is more vulnerable if the network is overpowered by an attacker. While network nodes can verify transactions for themselves, the simplified method can be fooled by an attacker's fabricated transactions for as long as the attacker can continue to overpower the network. One strategy to protect against this would be to accept alerts from network nodes when they detect an invalid block, prompting the user's software to download the full block and alerted transactions to confirm the inconsistency. Businesses that receive frequent payments will probably still want to run their own nodes for more independent security and quicker verification.

9. Combining and Splitting Value

Although it would be possible to handle coins individually, it would be unwieldy to make a separate transaction for every cent in a transfer. To allow value to be split and combined, transactions contain multiple inputs and outputs. Normally there will be either a single input from a larger previous transaction or multiple inputs combining smaller amounts, and at most two outputs: one for the payment, and one returning the change, if any, back to the sender.

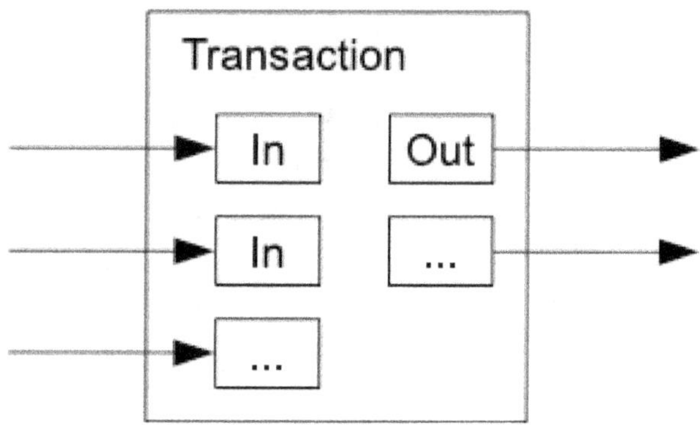

It should be noted that fan-out, where a transaction depends on several transactions, and those transactions depend on many more, is not a problem here. There is never the need to extract a complete standalone copy of a transaction's history.

10. Privacy

The traditional banking model achieves a level of privacy by limiting access to information to the parties involved and the trusted third party. The necessity to announce all transactions publicly precludes this method, but privacy can still be maintained by breaking the flow of information in another place: by keeping public keys anonymous. The public can see that someone is sending an amount to someone else, but without information linking the transaction to anyone. This is similar to the level of information released by stock exchanges, where the time and size of individual trades, the "tape", is made public, but without telling who the parties were.

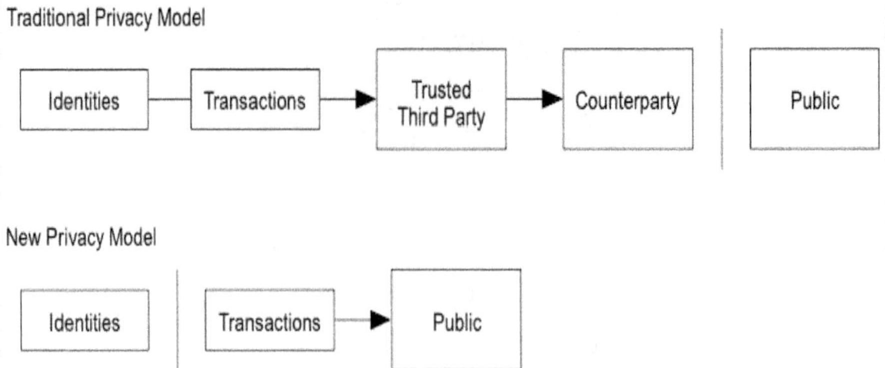

As an additional firewall, a new key pair should be used for each transaction to keep them from being linked to a common owner. Some linking is still unavoidable with multi-input transactions, which necessarily reveal that their inputs were owned by the same owner. The risk is that if the owner of a key is revealed, linking could reveal other transactions that belonged to the same owner.

11. Calculations

We consider the scenario of an attacker trying to generate an alternate chain faster than the honest chain. Even if this is accomplished, it does not throw the system open to arbitrary changes, such as creating value out of thin air or taking money that never belonged to the attacker. Nodes are not going to accept an invalid transaction as payment, and honest nodes will never accept a block containing them. An attacker can only try to change one of his own transactions to take back money he recently spent.

The race between the honest chain and an attacker chain can be characterized as a Binomial Random Walk. The success event is the honest chain being extended by one block, increasing its lead by +1, and the failure event is the attacker's chain being extended by one block, reducing the gap by -1.

The probability of an attacker catching up from a given deficit is analogous to a Gambler's Ruin problem. Suppose a gambler with unlimited credit starts at a deficit and plays potentially an infinite number of trials to try to reach breakeven. We can calculate the probability he ever reaches breakeven, or that an attacker ever catches up with the honest chain, as follows[8]:

pqqz=== probability an honest node finds the next block probability the attacker finds the next block probability the attacker will ever catch up from z blocks behind

qz={1(q/p)zifp≤qifp>q}��={1if�≤�(�/�)�if�>�}

Given our assumption that p>q, the probability drops exponentially as the number of blocks the attacker has to catch up with increases. With the odds against him, if he doesn't make a lucky lunge forward early on, his chances become vanishingly small as he falls further behind.

We now consider how long the recipient of a new transaction needs to wait before being sufficiently certain the sender can't change the transaction. We assume the sender is an attacker who wants to make the recipient believe he paid him for a while, then switch it to pay back to himself after some time has passed. The receiver will be alerted when that happens, but the sender hopes it will be too late.

The receiver generates a new key pair and gives the public key to the sender shortly before signing. This prevents the sender from preparing a chain of blocks ahead of time by working on it continuously until he is lucky enough to get far enough ahead, then executing the transaction at that moment. Once the transaction is sent, the dishonest sender starts working in secret on a parallel chain containing an alternate version of his transaction.

The recipient waits until the transaction has been added to a block and z blocks have been linked after it. He doesn't know the exact amount of progress the attacker has made, but assuming the honest blocks took the average expected time per block, the attacker's potential progress will be a Poisson distribution with expected value:

$$\lambda = z\frac{q}{p}$$

To get the probability the attacker could still catch up now, we multiply the Poisson density for each amount of progress he could have made by the probability he could catch up from that point:

$$\sum_{k=0}^{\infty} \frac{\lambda^k e^{-\lambda}}{k!} \cdot \begin{cases} (q/p)^{(z-k)} & \text{if } k \le z \\ 1 & \text{if } k > z \end{cases}$$

Rearranging to avoid summing the infinite tail of the distribution...

$$1 - \sum_{k=0}^{z} \frac{\lambda^k e^{-\lambda}}{k!} \left(1 - (q/p)^{(z-k)}\right)$$

Converting to C code...

```c
#include <math.h>

double AttackerSuccessProbability(double q, int z)
{
        double p = 1.0 - q;
        double lambda = z * (q / p);
        double sum = 1.0;
        int i, k;
        for (k = 0; k <= z; k++)
        {
                double poisson = exp(-lambda);
                for (i = 1; i <= k; i++)
                        poisson *= lambda / i;
                sum -= poisson * (1 - pow(q / p, z - k));
        }
        return sum;
}
```

Running some results, we can see the probability drop off exponentially with z.

```
q=0.1
z=0   P=1.0000000
z=1   P=0.2045873
z=2   P=0.0509779
z=3   P=0.0131722
z=4   P=0.0034552
z=5   P=0.0009137
```

z=6   P=0.0002428
z=7   P=0.0000647
z=8   P=0.0000173
z=9   P=0.0000046
z=10   P=0.0000012

q=0.3
z=0   P=1.0000000
z=5   P=0.1773523
z=10   P=0.0416605
z=15   P=0.0101008
z=20   P=0.0024804
z=25   P=0.0006132
z=30   P=0.0001522
z=35   P=0.0000379
z=40   P=0.0000095
z=45   P=0.0000024
z=50   P=0.0000006
Solving for P less than 0.1%...
P < 0.001
q=0.10   z=5
q=0.15   z=8
q=0.20   z=11
q=0.25   z=15
q=0.30   z=24
q=0.35   z=41

q=0.40 z=89

q=0.45 z=340

1 2 .   C o n c l u s i o n

We have proposed a system for electronic transactions without relying on trust. We started with the usual framework of coins made from digital signatures, which provides strong control of ownership, but is incomplete without a way to prevent double-spending. To solve this, we proposed a peer-to-peer network using proof-of-work to record a public history of transactions that quickly becomes computationally impractical for an attacker to change if honest nodes control a majority of CPU power. The network is robust in its unstructured simplicity. Nodes work all at once with little coordination. They do not need to be identified, since messages are not routed to any particular place and only need to be delivered on a best effort basis. Nodes can leave and rejoin the network at will, accepting the proof-of-work chain as proof of what happened while they were gone. They vote with their CPU power, expressing their acceptance of valid blocks by working on extending them and rejecting invalid blocks by refusing to work on them. Any needed rules and incentives can be enforced with this consensus mechanism.